I0760025

Decking the Halls

Decking the Halls

Trees, Flowers, Herbs & Greenery to Celebrate the Holiday Season

JANET MELROSE &
SHERYL NORMANDEAU

TOUCHWOOD

TouchWood Editions
Touchwoodeditions.com

The information in this book is true and complete to the best of the authors' knowledge. All recommendations are made without guarantee on the part of the authors or the publisher.

Copy edited by Kaiya Cade Smith Blackburn
Proofread by Senica Maltese
Illustrations, cover, and interior design by Jazmin Welch

CATALOGUING DATA AVAILABLE FROM LIBRARY AND ARCHIVES CANADA

ISBN 9781771514637 (hardcover)
ISBN 9781771514644 (epub)

TouchWood Editions gratefully acknowledges that the land on which we live and work is within the traditional territories of the Lkwungen (Esquimalt and Songhees), Malahat, Pacheedaht, Scia'new, T'Sou-ke and W̱SÁNEĆ (Pauquachin, Tsartlip, Tsawout, Tseycum) peoples.

We acknowledge the financial support of the Government of Canada through the Canada Book Fund and the Canada Council for the Arts, and of the Province of British Columbia through the British Columbia Arts Council and the Book Publishing Tax Credit.

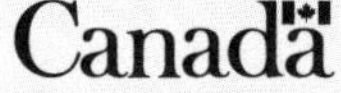

This book was produced using FSC®-certified, acid-free papers, processed chlorine free, and printed with soya-based inks.

Printed in China

29 28 27 26 25 1 2 3 4 5

To all those gardeners who never hang up their trowels and celebrate the season by bringing in the greens this time of year.

TABLE OF CONTENTS

Introduction

As gardeners, how do we mark the change of seasons? Spring is hectic with seed sowing and enjoying the lively return of birds and insects and perennial blooms. The world is filled with sound and colour, and the soil is warm in our hands. In the summer, we spend hours on our knees weeding. We lug watering cans around the garden and watch our plants as they mature. We harvest fresh delights such as green peas and crisp beans, and bring the flowers of zinnias and lisianthus into our dining rooms. Our evenings are spent on lawn chairs, enjoying the fragrance of evening-scented stock and lavender. In autumn, we clamber to get the pumpkins in before the heavy frosts and watch deciduous leaves change colour and fall to the ground. For us in cold climates, the growing season always seems shorter than we would like—suddenly, it's over for the year, with beds tucked away under a covering of mulch and the tools hung up in the shed. Gardeners anxiously anticipate the shortest day of the year, for its arrival means that we are in a time of renewal and rebirth as we celebrate the upcoming festive season and the return of the light. Spring is not far away!

You might be forgiven for thinking that there is nothing left to do in the winter but tend our houseplants. But fear not, there is a whole other gardening season at this time of year. Whether it is growing an amaryllis or planting up a holiday planter with poinsettia, ivy, and holly, there is plenty to do. Bringing in the greens is an ancient practice at this time of year where we decorate our homes with wreaths, garlands, arrangements, and more. Then there is the tree to be the focal point of our homes for the Twelve Days of Christmas. Festive baking and cooking with all those spices and herbs fills the house with smells that evoke Christmases long gone.

This season is one filled with poignant memories, ongoing traditions, and a wealth of meanings as we celebrate the turn of the year by drawing on centuries of symbolism and practices. As you read about these traditions and beliefs through history and across cultures, you'll recognize a pattern: humans need to bring colour, light, and peace into our lives during dark times. From the warmth of the yule log to the significance of Persephone's pomegranate, from the Druidic rituals surrounding the oak tree to the Arthurian connection to Glastonbury thorn, hope and renewal are themes that run through all these stories, and plants are a huge part of the cycle.[1]

Join us as we explore the world of gardening in the dead of winter!

—Janet and Sheryl

SOLSTICE SCIENCE

We're focusing on the Northern Hemisphere in this book, so when we are talking about the winter or hibernal solstice, we're referring to the moment when the sun's path in the sky is the farthest south it can be in the Northern Hemisphere. That is, of course, due to the fact that the Earth rotates on a tilted axis as it revolves around the sun. This happens on December 20 or 21 each year (and while we're having the shortest day of the year here, the day with the fewest daylight hours, the Southern Hemisphere is experiencing their longest day of the year as their half of the planet is pointed toward the sun). On the day of the winter solstice, the sun's path in the sky is as low as it will be at any other point in the year. It's so low on the horizon that the name *solstice* means "sun/stand still" in Latin.

The hibernal solstice marks the start of the astronomical winter, but in case you're wondering, the meteorological winter has already been in full swing for about three weeks by the time the solstice rolls around. That's the range on the calendar from December 1 to the end of February that bases the duration of winter on temperatures and climate. No matter how you measure it, by December there are signs everywhere that winter has arrived and with it, the darkness and, for many, the cold. —SN

Chapter 1.

The TREES, SHRUBS, and PERENNIALS of the SEASON

Throughout the ages, people have considered certain plants sacred. Myths and legends have grown up around them. They are revered and used in rituals and ceremonies that span the centuries and all cultures.

Here are a few of the special trees, shrubs, and perennials associated with the special time of year that is the winter solstice, Christmas, and the twelve days of celebrations that take us into the new year and the return of the light.

THE YULE LOG

An Ancient Symbol of Winter

The yule log has its origin in ancient Germanic and Scandinavian celebrations of the winter solstice. In Celtic traditions, it was believed that the sun stood still for the twelve days after the solstice.[2] Lighting the yule log both symbolized the divine light and encouraged the sun to move again and bring the renewal of the earth.

By medieval times, the custom evolved into hewing an oak or other large tree and bringing either the entire tree or a large log into the house on Christmas Day. The log was placed with great ceremony in the hearth and lit with the remnants of the previous years' yule log, which would ensure prosperity and good fortune for the coming year. The log would be kept alight for the entire twelve days of Christmas and be extinguished on the twelfth night. The remains of the log and its ashes were gathered up, and the ashes kept to spread on the fields in spring for good luck and for the harvest to come. The charred remains of the log were often kept under a bed for good luck.

These days, few of us have a hearth big enough to hold a large log—or, for that matter, a hearth at all. You can make your own yule log, using a small log with holes drilled in it to hold candles, and decorated with evergreen foliage, cones, and spices. The same wish for prosperity and good fortune accompanies the lighting of this simple yule log even in these modern days.

Of course, you can also bring the yule log in as a very fancy dessert called Bûche de Noël. It is a light sponge cake spread with a cream filling and rolled up to make a log. Frosting the log with chocolate icing and decorating it extravagantly adds a special touch to modern-day celebrations of the season. And you don't have to spread the ashes on your garden beds![3] —JM

OAK TREE
The Mighty One

The oak (*Quercus* spp.) is a hardwood tree in the beech family, Fagaceae, which was the preferred species for the yule log. Oak trees have long been sacred, with Druids worshipping in oak groves. The oak has been venerated by many cultures besides the Celts, from the ancient Greeks and Romans to Teutonic and Slavic peoples. The oak is often the tallest tree in the landscape and subject to lightning strikes and as such is associated with thunder gods such as Zeus, Jupiter, and Thor. Kings would wear oak crowns to symbolize their power and responsibility for both their land and their peoples.[4]

The oak genus has some 500 species distributed around the Northern Hemisphere. They are often keystone species in many ecosystems, and hosts for mistletoe and many caterpillars. Slow growers, they are often very large and long-lived. They have corky, grey bark and spirally arranged leaves that are deeply lobed. Their fruit is an acorn or nut, held in a cup-shaped receptacle called a cupule.

The magnificent oak, dominant in its landscape, is worthy of being a yule log, a symbol of the waxing sun that represents endurance, strength, and protection.[5] —JM

BIRCH
New Beginnings

Birch trees are symbols for the awakening of new life, rebirth, and the cycle of life. In the Ogham, the Celtic Tree Calendar, the silver birch (*Betula pendula*) is the tree for the lunar month between December 24 and January 20. In Nordic mythology, birch trees had magical properties. In Scotland, a birch tree was the favoured choice for the yule log.

In North America, Indigenous peoples valued birch trees as guardians of people, providing protection and new beginnings. As one of the first trees to repopulate an area after fire, it is the "tree of new beginnings."[6]

Birch (*Betula* spp.) are small- to medium-sized shrubs and trees, reaching up to some sixty-six feet (twenty metres) and taller. They are known for their thin, white bark with long, black, horizontal lenticels that readily peel away in strips. The paper birch (*B. papyrifera*), which is native to Canada and the northern United States, is most notable for this distinctive quality. Birch leaves are simple, serrated and appear in twos on short branchlets. The shining yellow-gold leaves are simply stunning against the white bark in fall.

Birch bark and wood is used extensively for making canoes, tools, and structures. The bark is also used medicinally and even as an emergency food. It can be used extensively for decorating our homes and celebrating the season. A simple log of birch can be a symbolic yule log, with or without holes drilled into one side to hold candles. Birch logs and twigs are also very popular in seasonal arrangements with other greens. A small birch tree can be cut to make a Christmas tree with a difference. The bark can be used to make ornaments. Lastly, bases for tree ornaments can be made by cutting the logs into wood cookies. Alternatively, you can drill a hole in the bottom of the wood cookies, insert a skewer, and glue it into place to make great ornaments for arrangements. Only our imaginations limit how we can use birch with its symbolism of renewal in our seasonal celebrations. —JM

THE GLASTONBURY THORN

A Hawthorn with Special Significance

The region near the town of Glastonbury, England is home to a cultivar of hawthorn tree (*Crataegus monogyna* 'Biflora') that blooms in May and then flowers again around the time of the winter solstice. Repeat blooms are not usual for most hawthorn species, so this must have caused quite a stir among early Christians in the area—and, indeed, the connection to the observation of the birth of Jesus is still celebrated nowadays when the brilliant white flowers appear. (Horticulturally speaking, 'Biflora' is likely a naturally occurring sport of common hawthorn.)

But it's not simply the collective of hawthorn trees that is important in Glastonbury. One, in particular, has been imbued with special significance. Legend has it that Joseph of Arimathea, the uncle of the Virgin Mary (and, incidentally, the disciple that readied the tomb of Jesus) made a trek to Glastonbury at some point in his lifetime, and he happened to visit the Glastonbury Tor, a hill with long-held mythical power as the resting place of King Arthur and Queen Guinevere (and which was also a sacred site for Druidic worshippers). Joseph planted his wooden staff into the ground of the Tor, and from it grew the Glastonbury Thorn. The earliest documented case of the Thorn blooming in the wintertime is in 1535, and the original Thorn supposedly planted by Joseph of Arimathea was destroyed in 1653 during the English Civil War. The tree was replaced by a new one in 1952 to honour the ascension of Queen Elizabeth II to the throne. That tree was gruesomely vandalized in 2010, and another tree was planted in 2022 and dedicated to King Charles III. While the original story of the Thorn is not verifiable, the beauty and the religious symbolism of the blooms make them an important holiday tradition.

If you're looking to bring a few spring blooms into your home during the bleak wintertime, you can *force* the blooms from the trees in your garden. Give your spring-flowering trees and shrubs a cold period of at least six weeks to get them ready for forcing, then go out into the garden with a sharp pair of secateurs and trim away a few of the minor branches. Bring the branches indoors and arrange them in a tall vase filled with water. Refresh the water every couple of days and wait for the magic to happen—depending on the plant you are forcing, it can take anywhere from one week to two months for blooms to appear. Plants that work well for this treatment include cherry, forsythia, tulip magnolia, flowering almond, lilac, and pussy willow (the latter will bloom even without water!).[7]–SN

The *Holly* and the *Ivy*

Holly (*Ilex* spp.) and ivy (*Hedera* spp.) have been immortalized in Christmas tradition through the carol or folk song "The Holly and the Ivy." Dating back to the early 1800s, this iconic English song depicts holly as the Christ Child and ivy as the Virgin Mary. The song honours the masculine and feminine in tandem, with holly representing the male and ivy the female. The rivalry between holly and ivy is represented as well in the games of forfeit between genders, and participants would sing rude songs about the other gender at midwinter celebrations.

Venturing further into the mists of myth, ivy has been a symbol of fidelity, fertility, and immortality in many cultures and civilizations. The ancient Egyptians associated ivy with Osiris, the god of fertility and ruler of the underworld. In ancient Greece and Rome, ivy was the plant of Dionysus and Baccus, the gods of wine and mirth but also fertility. As matter of interest, wearing an ivy garland like these gods was supposed to ward off the effects of too much wine or ale. . . perhaps a result of too much mirth?

Across the Northern Hemisphere and across time, ivy has represented eternal life as an evergreen with magical powers that enables mankind to withstand the rigors of dark and cold winters while providing hope of spring returning.

Further back, our pagan ancestors looked at the growing habits of ivy for the symbolism it represents. Ivy starts off as a groundcover, but when it encounters a vertical structure such as a tree, it begins to climb it, spiraling around it and heading toward the light. This spiraling nature became associated with the immortal sun, who rotates through the sky daily, dipping and weaving through the seasons, yet always reappearing as a sign of rebirth, be it the new day or the new season. —JM

HOLLY
A Plant of Seasonal (and Spiritual) Renewal

Broadleaf evergreens such as European holly (*Ilex aquifolium*) are indisputable choices to bring indoors during bleak, cold winters: their perpetual brilliant green colour is an affirmation that spring is never far away. While we associate holly with western Christmas traditions, its use to celebrate the bounty of the harvest and the onset of winter has much older origins. The ancient Roman festival of Saturnalia, which honoured Saturn, the god of agriculture, abundant harvests, and renewal, took place just before the winter solstice. During this week-long fête, all Roman citizens regardless of class took a holiday from work and dedicated their time to partying. Gifts were exchanged (sound familiar?), trimmed with fresh cut holly as a symbol of good fortune. People hung wreaths and garlands of holly both inside and outside of their homes and public spaces. Trust in the positive benefits of the plant was so widely accepted that eventually enterprising entrepreneurs started marketing holly as a way to cure diseases.

When followers of the newly founded religion of Christianity faced deadly persecution by the Romans, they secretly attached a different significance to the holly of Saturnalia. Instead, the thorns found on the margins of the leaves became representative of the crown of thorns that Christ wore during his crucifixion. Holly's red fruit were thought to represent drops of blood. (By the way, those berry-like fruit are actually drupes. Other fruit plants that bear drupes include peaches, plums, and cherries.) The plant symbolized the sacrifice of Jesus and the renewal that was brought forth by the resurrection. Four hundred years later, as Christianity became the dominant religion in Rome, the old pagan beliefs and the new religion were amalgamated, with holly remaining one of the links between the past and the present.

In another part of what is now Europe, the Druids in Celtic Britain used holly as the subject of an important legend about the constant battle between the Oak King and the Holly King, both of whom wanted to rule the forests. The Holly King of course was the clearcut winner during the wintertime, as the deciduous Oak King lost all his leaves and could not compete. Holly was considered imbued with power, and Celts brought it into their homes to help protect them from evil.

English folklore gives holly the power to ward off witches (although, in a strange twist, witches were fond of making magical wands out of holly because apparently the wood made spellcasting more reliable. The most famous wizard of modern fiction, Harry Potter, has a holly wand.) It was said that bad luck would befall you if you discarded holly improperly after putting it up as decorations. It had to be burned, not simply tossed out. It is interesting to note that early Christians believed that the wood from holly trees was used to build the cross upon which Jesus was sacrificed.

Even Norse mythology references holly, describing it as a favoured plant belonging to Thor, god of thunder. Indigenous cultures such as the Catawba in southeastern North America used leaves from *I. vomitoria* (Yaupon holly) as a drink and as a product of trade.

The genus *Ilex* has over 400 species and not all of them are evergreen. European holly is native to regions in west and south Europe, as well as northwest Africa and southwest Asia. This is the plant we most commonly associate with Christmas, with its glossy green, prickly leaves and shiny, bright red berries. American holly (*I. opaca*), which has dull green leaves and berries that lack the lustre of its European counterpart, is native to a wide distribution in North America. American holly cannot tolerate extreme cold, so it is not found in northern Canada. European holly has been introduced to North America as well, but it grows so vigorously in warmer climates that it is considered an invasive species in many areas, particularly in the eastern United States.

Cultivated European holly trees grown in their native habitat can reach fifty feet (fifteen metres) or more in height. (Wild ones don't usually grow quite as tall.) If they are happy where they are growing, they can easily live to a century or several: the oldest holly on record is in Spain and is a whopping 600 years old. American holly will slowly grow to a similar height and has an attractive pyramidal form. If you're not interested in growing a tree, choose other holly plants (or holly relatives) that are shrubby in form, such as Chinese holly (*I. cornuta*), common winterberry (*I. verticillate*), or catberry (*I. mucronata*).

Most holly plants prefer full sun, but they will happily tolerate part shade as well. Species such as common winterberry require plenty of moisture to thrive, while species like Chinese holly can be quite drought tolerant once established. Be prepared to do some research before planting holly and check the invasive species list in your region. They might not be welcome where you live!

Many, but not all, holly plants are dioecious, which means they require both a female and a male plant to bear fruit. If you are looking for the very best holiday decorations, that beautiful fruit will be important, so make sure you plan for it when selecting plants at the garden centre. Remember, too, that the berries are toxic and not safe for consumption by humans or pets. Many species of birds will happily chow down on them, however, so don't throw away your decorations after the season is over![8]—SN

IVY

Symbol of Fidelity and Immortality

Ivy belongs to the genus *Hedera*, part of the family Araliaceae. It is a small genus of some twelve to fifteen species, of which common or English ivy (*Hedera helix*) is the most commonly grown species for our gardens and homes. As a groundcover, ivy usually grows no taller than two to eight inches (five to twenty centimetres) as it trails along the ground. Yet it can reach some ninety feet (thirty metres) as it grows up the side of a building or spirals around a tree. The leaves are five-lobed as juveniles but with maturity are cordate or heart shaped. The shoots have small aerial roots that allow the stems to affix to the surface of rock or bark, enabling the plant to scale the heights. For those who live in milder climes, ivy will develop small greenish-yellow, five-petalled flowers come late autumn that are a nectar bomb for pollinators. The flowers develop into greenish-black berries that are a great source of food for birds and the plant's main method of seed dispersal.

Ivy has a bit of a bad rap in southern areas where it can become invasive. While not parasitic in nature, ivy can overwhelm trees to the point of smothering them with their foliage. The aerial roots will not break brick walls but will take advantage of any fissures in the brick as they clamber upward.

Ivy is often grown inside year-round as a houseplant where it enjoys the conditions prevailing in our homes. Though if we were living in times passed, it would be considered bad luck to do so. The tradition was to only bring in ivy on Christmas Eve, where it would ward off evil spirits and be a source of good fortune. But it would need to be burned by Twelfth Night, or the good luck would become bad luck.

Ivy is often included in live holiday arrangements with other celebratory plants. It can also be used with other greenery as a living wreath or wound around a twig wreath. However, if you include ivy in your mid-winter decorating be sure to reflect on its powerful symbolic role in our collective heritage.[9] —JM

MISTLETOE
A Mystical Plant

Mistletoe is an ancient plant that today we in North America associate with being hung in a doorway, so that anyone passing under the plant receives a kiss. In days gone by, that kiss would, of course, lead to marriage!

The origins of this modern-day usage can be traced back to Nordic mythology. The Norse god of peace and light, Balder, was killed by an arrow made of mistletoe by the blind god Hud at the instigation of the trickster Loki. For love of Balder, his parents Odin and Frigga restored Balder to life and gave mistletoe to the goddess of love, Freya. From this legend mistletoe came to symbolize both peace and love. Hence the kissing ball of mistletoe.

Mistletoe was also a powerful symbol in Druidic traditions, in which sprigs of the plant were cut with a golden knife at midsummer and midwinter. In ancient Greece and Rome, mistletoe was hung from doorways as a symbol of peace, love, and fertility.

By the Middle Ages, mistletoe was also hung over doorways to ward off evil spirits and witches. It was also considered an aphrodisiac with life-protecting powers. Indeed, mistletoe has for centuries been used medicinally for a variety of conditions ranging from epilepsy to arthritis and from headaches to infertility. It now shows promise in the treatment of cancer.

So, what exactly is mistletoe with its rich lore, traditions, and mystical powers? Mistletoe is named from the Anglo-Saxon *mistel* (meaning dung) and *tan* (meaning twig) due to the belief that it grew in trees where bird droppings would accumulate. This is an astute naming, though mistaken, as it was the seeds of mistletoe contained in the dung that would attach to a tree and so propagate there. Mistletoes are a group of parasites or hemiparasites from three families, Loranthaceae, Misodendraceae, and Santalaceae. There are about 1,500 species that are all named mistletoe, but the one we most commonly associate with these myths and traditions is European mistletoe (*Viscum alba*).

Mistletoes arise in treetops when the sticky seeds land on the bark of a healthy, mature tree. After the seeds germinate, they send out a modified root, called the haustorium, which penetrates the bark of the tree, allowing nutrients and water pass from the host tree to the growing mistletoe shrub. Over time, a sizeable witch's broom, some two to three feet (sixty to ninety centimetres) will be firmly attached to the tree. Mistletoe bears broadleaf evergreen leaves and loads of white sticky berries. Being hemiparasites, mistletoe does contain chlorophyll and can photosynthesize. Mistletoe does not kill a tree, but can weaken it, especially if there are a number of growths present. The berries are poisonous to animals, but not to birds who will eat them copiously, thus dispersing the seeds around to infect even more trees.

In Canada, most mistletoes are not to be found as our winters are too harsh for them. Dwarf mistletoes, in the genus *Arceuthobium*, are another matter, with four species native to Canada. Dwarf mistletoe is fully established in southern British Columbia and parasitize spruce, pine, and Douglas fir. Mistletoe also functions as a home and source of food for bees, butterflies, and birds.

As part of the age-old tradition of bringing in the greens to decorate our homes at this time of year, it's not a bad idea to have a plant associated with peace, love, and healing inside with us all.[10] —JM

THE CHRISTMAS ROSE
Symbol of Purity and Love

The Christmas rose is the story of a poor shepherd girl who goes to see the Christ Child. The Magi appear with their magnificent gifts, along with worshipping shepherds and their gifts of fruit, honey, and doves. She stands by the doorway and cries for love of the babe but has no gift to give. An angel spots her standing there and turns her tears of love into the white petals of a beautiful plant that has bloomed for the first time ever, the Christmas rose. She gathers the flowers and presents them at the manger where the babe reaches out to receive them, ignoring the rich and exotic gifts of the Magi.

Ever since, the Christmas rose, or black hellebore (*Helleborus niger*) has been a symbol for pure love. It is also the only herbaceous perennial that blooms during the winter months from December through April, giving rise to its other names, the 'Snow Rose' or 'Winter Rose.'[11] In northern climates where winters are biting and the snow lies deep, the Christmas rose blooms come spring, though in my garden it bloomed in February one unseasonably warm winter to my immense delight.

Not a rose at all, *Helleborus* is a genus in the buttercup family, Ranunculaceae. The plant is considered one of the most noble, with dark green, leathery compound leaves that are evergreen in warm climates. Arising from the crown are stalks with large flat, five-petalled flowers that are white with a tinge of pink surrounding a large centre with multiple stamens.

The Christmas rose is native to both the Southern and Northern Alps, as well as the Apennines and into the mountains of the Balkans. As with most buttercup species, hellebore is poisonous if consumed. It also has a rich tradition of medicinal use, and the petals have been placed around homes to ward off evil spirits.

The Christmas rose is also called the Flower of St. Agnes, after a thirteen-year-old girl martyred for her faith.[12] Her feast day is January 21 when this marvelous plant is in full bloom in its native home. —JM

WINTERGREEN

A Northern Plant to Warm Your Holiday Home

Native to northeastern North America, creeping wintergreen (*Gaultheria procumbens*), with its low, shrubby evergreen growth habit and beautiful prolific red, edible (and surprisingly mint-flavoured) berries are a delightful addition to the holiday house-plant repertoire. The leaves also taste like mint and are often used in tisanes. As the leaves are evergreen, they've come to symbolize good health, and the plant is connected to both Saturn and the moon, which supposedly imbue it with the power to protect and heal. It is said that carrying a piece of wintergreen on your person will ward off evil. Indigenous peoples across North America, such as the Haudenosaunee and the Anishinaabe, used wintergreen medicinally to combat a wide range of ailments, another extension of its healing and protective power.

With all these things already going for the plant, wintergreen requires about as little care as you could ask for. Forget the diva-esque antics of poinsettias (they are tropical and can't help but swoon when they get into our dry, furnace-hot winter homes). Wintergreen plants prefer part shade so they're not angling for the sun like many of your houseplants are. They do like a fair amount of humidity which you are likely offering some of your other houseplants, anyway. Go easy on the watering, as the plants don't enjoy boggy conditions (but don't let them dry out too much between waterings, either!). Over time, you'll need to consider the pH of your growing medium, as wintergreen plants—being related to rhododendrons—prefer slightly acidic soil. But for a month or two out of the year, this isn't going to matter much, and when you transplant wintergreen outdoors in the spring, you can ensure they have the soil conditions they require.

Another very compact wintergreen you may happen upon is the Japanese cultivar called 'Winter Fiesta,' a plant characterized by white berries that turn pink in the winter. Another cultivar, 'Winter Splash,' has unique variegated foliage. Both can be grown outdoors in Canadian hardiness zone 3, as can *G. procumbens*. If you live in the correct zone, you are safe to turn the plants out into the ground in the spring should you no longer wish to keep them inside.

Set diminutive wintergreen plants in sparkly containers among fresh boughs of fir or pine and tall potted herbs such as rosemary for a gorgeous fragrant holiday mantlepiece. Then enjoy the show![13] —SN

Chapter 2.

BRINGING in the GREENS: DECORATING the HOME

THE CHRISTMAS TREE

How the Vikings, a Bold Saint, a German Clergyman, and the British Monarchy Started a Custom Celebrated Worldwide

One of my favourite childhood memories is the annual car trip to the woods to select and cut a conifer to be used as a Christmas tree. Back then (let's just vaguely say it was a while ago), there was a lot of snow in northern Alberta, and my parents would pack the long wooden toboggan so my brother and I could be pulled along while they looked for a tree that was a suitable size and shape for our living room. My favourite thing about having a fresh-cut Christmas tree has always been that incredible fragrance, composed of special chemicals such as pinene and limonene that I can't get enough of.

How did we get to this idea of bringing a tree into our homes during the holiday season? Traditions associated with bringing evergreens indoors exist across many cultures. The yule log, evergreen wreaths, and other decorations displayed during the Roman festival of Saturnalia are common examples. Evergreens, with needles that stay green through the whole year, bring us closer to the natural world, especially in the wintertime, when our bodies and minds are craving light, warmth, and serenity. That's exactly what inspired the Vikings to bring felled fir trees into their homes as the bitter winds howled and the snow piles grew in Scandinavia in the Middle Ages. Evergreen trees were resilient, thriving even when winter served up its worst, and it was fitting to share in and be bolstered by some of that enchantment.

The custom of the Christmas tree didn't begin to take hold until the seventh century, when an English monk, the man who would become St. Boniface, encountered a group of pagans in his travels through western Europe. They were worshipping an oak tree and preparing to sacrifice a young child. Boniface was intolerant of the ritual and told the men to stop. To drive his point home, Boniface hit the oak tree with his fist. (In other accounts, he chopped it down with an axe he seized from the men.) The massive tree crashed to the ground. Behind the oak tree was a small fir tree, which Boniface christened "The Tree of Life," as an evergreen is eternal despite the weather and the season. To complete his lesson, Boniface told the men that the tree's triangular shape represented the Holy Trinity. Needless to say, no one was sacrificed that day. The story of Boniface's encounter spread throughout France and Germany and over the next five centuries, Christmas trees were hung upside-down from the ceilings of homes as a symbol of the Trinity.

Until the German Protestant Reformer Martin Luther decided in the 1500s that Christmas trees required a little candlelight to make them shine, however, they were not widespread holiday decor. Once Christmas trees were sparkling with light, their popularity in Germany soared. Luther emphasized that the tree was a symbol of the perpetual nature of God's love, and the candles were the hope represented by the birth of Jesus. The idea became everlasting.

Although Queen Charlotte and King George III had set up a Christmas tree at Windsor Castle in the late eighteenth century, Christmas trees didn't become trendy until Prince Albert (who was German) and Queen Victoria of England brought a Christmas tree to the royal palace in 1841. The English people responded with immense favour, as did the Americans overseas. Christmas trees became hugely popular. In fact, in less than fifty years, enterprising American entrepreneurs were erecting Christmas tree lots and certain species of fir trees were already becoming scarce.

What about all the decorations we now carefully stow away eleven months of the year? Prince Albert, Queen Victoria, and their children decorated their trees with spiced gingerbread and fruit, and by the 1920s, North American trees were festooned with delicate blown glass ornaments, popcorn chains, and cranberry garlands, as well as metal tinsel and electric lights (holiday fire safety was clearly becoming a priority by then). During the Great Depression and the Second World War, handmade and upcycled ornaments were fashioned from fabric, paper, and other bits and bobs.

Nowadays, real and artificial Christmas trees of all shapes and sizes (including the iconic and much-loved Charlie Brown tree inspired by Charles M. Schulz's Peanuts holiday special, which originally aired in 1965) are found in homes all over North America and the rest of the world. The idea of the tree as a symbol of eternal life and light in the darkness transcends culture and religion. (Martin Luther never could have envisioned our LED lights that can be connected to Wi-Fi.) Even upside-down Christmas trees have made a comeback in the past decade, ostensibly because they are space-saving in small homes! But I still love the scent of those fresh-cut trees most of all.[14] —SN

The Christmas Trees

of North America

BALSAM FIR

Balsam fir (*Abies balsamea*) is a wonderful Christmas tree that is native to North America from northern Alberta east to Labrador and south to the northeastern United States. It is a very cold-hardy tree that can be found in elevations as high as 5,000 feet (1,524 metres) and all the way down to sea level.

The species gets its name from the resinous blisters found on the bark of young trees, which also provides the species' alternative name, blister pine. That resin is called *Canada balsam* and is used for glue, scented soaps, and candles as well as being the source for microscope slides.

Balsam fir has been used by North American Indigenous peoples throughout the ages to relieve pain, heal wounds, and act as an antiseptic and diuretic. The young needles are edible and nutritious, often steeped as a tea or eaten as a green by humans and wildlife alike.

This tree has a lovely conical or narrow pyramidal shape and dark green, dense foliage. The soft, highly scented needles are flat with two white bands on the bottom with disks or balls where they attach to branches, providing a clue to the name *balsam*. The needles are ⅝–1⅛ inches (15–30 milimetres) long and are arranged spirally, twisting to form two horizontal rows on either side of the twig, making the foliage appear flat.

To many people, especially in eastern North America, balsam fir is *the* Christmas tree, and not just for the wonderful scent that comes from its volatile oils, called *pinenes*, which evaporate when it is warm. These oils repel insects, but they are attractive to us. The branches are also beautifully spaced for candles, creating enough room for the flame to burn without setting the tree on fire.[15] Thankfully, we don't have lit candles in our tree these days, but those widely spaced branches allow for lots and lots of decorations! Whenever I have had a balsam tree for Christmas, it usually lasts upward of five weeks with care, and I love it every minute it is in my home.[16] —JM

CONCOLOR FIR

The concolor or white fir (*Abies concolor*) is a Christmas tree with a difference. What makes it a standout among firs is its soft blue-green to blue-silver needles that have a distinct citrusy aroma. Native to the western United States, the concolor fir can reach 130–150 feet (40–46 metres) tall if left to mature and often has a spire-like crown with a bare trunk below. In a tree farm, where they are grown to a more appropriate size for our homes, they have a narrow pyramidical shape with the branches arranged in an open spiral. The narrow needles are longer than most firs, around 1–1 ½ inches (2.54–3.81 centimetres) long, and are arranged in rows. They have excellent needle retention once the tree has been cut and brought indoors. Definitely an elegant and unusual tree to grace your home during the festive season![17] —JM

DOUGLAS FIR

Douglas fir (*Pseudotsuga menziesii*) is named after David Douglas, a Scottish botanist and collector. It has been a go-to for Christmas trees and greens for western Canadians and Americans for decades.

Not actually a fir species, though belonging to the pine family, Pinaceae, Douglas fir belongs to its own genus, *Pseudotsuga,* which literally means false hemlock.[18] So, both its scientific and common name describe what it is not, rather than what it is!

In the wild, Douglas fir is a very large tree, with heights reaching between 70 and 330 feet (20 and 100 metres), especially

the coastal Douglas fir (*Pseudotsuga menziesii* var. *menziesii*). They are also very long lived, regularly surviving up to 500 years, with the oldest being some 1,300 years old. They are native to the Rocky Mountains and Pacific coastal regions from Alaska down through California.[19]

These days, Douglas fir destined for our homes are grown in tree farms, and the juvenile trees are harvested for Christmas trees and greens. What makes Douglas fir attractive is the soft, flat, yellow-green needles, which are ¾–1½ inches (2–4 centimetres) long. The single needles (not occurring in fascicles or bundles) encircle the twigs and are fragrant. So too is the bark of young trees as it usually has resin blisters growing on it. The needles can be delicate and may not remain attached for long, especially if there was drought the year they were harvested.

The branches are not strong or stiff, which makes hanging heavy ornaments on them problematic. Yet they are nicely spaced with lots of room to load up the tree with your favourites. In arrangements, Douglas fir is useful as a filler and emits a lovely citrusy aroma.

My heart has a soft spot for Douglas fir. After coming to Canada from places where there were no live Christmas trees, Douglas fir was always the tree that graced our home. —JM

FRASER FIR

Fraser fir (*Abies fraseri*) is native to the mountainous regions of the eastern United States and cultivated throughout the northern States and in the province of Quebec, Canada. Botanically speaking, the debate continues as to whether fraser fir is a subspecies of balsam fir (*A. balsamea*), but for the purposes of decorating your home for the holidays, it likely doesn't matter. Fraser fir has that signature citrus-mint scent that is beloved by so many, and it features a narrower growth habit than grand fir, which may be a desirable trait when it comes to setting up a tree in a small room. The dark green needles have an attractive, slightly blue cast, and the best part about them is that they are very long-lasting: you'll likely get up to six weeks without significant drop, which is easy on your vacuum cleaner and on your holiday celebrations.[20]—SN

GRAND FIR

Grand fir is one of the more expensive Christmas tree options out there due to the time it takes to grow (fraser fir will beat it in a race!), but, like fraser fir, it has attractive long-lasting needles. The needles of grand fir are up to 2.4 inches (6 centimetres) long, with a waxy silver sheen on the bottom edge that lends the appearance of sparkly fresh snow. In Canada, grand fir is native to the interior and coast of British Columbia and prefers consistently damp soil.[21]—SN

SCOT'S PINE

Scot's pine (*Pinus sylvestris*) is a non-native conifer that is considered—gasp!—an invasive species in some parts of Canada because this introduced tree is so incredibly successful that it out-competes native species. (In very cold parts of Canada, such as the prairie provinces, the species is checked by the winter temperatures.) When the major forests of Canada were logged a little too aggressively in the 1920s and 1930s, forestry managers frantically worried about the economic impact of a drastic reduction in product. Thus, they introduced a species they could easily import from Scotland and other parts of Europe as well as Asia. When Scot's pine hit Canadian soil, the trees did help immensely with protecting soils from erosion and contributing to reforestation efforts, but they loved their new pest-free environment and decided to conquer every inch, to the detriment of endemic conifers.

While you may have to exercise caution depending on where you live in Canada if you want to plant a Scot's pine in your yard, it makes a fantastic Christmas tree. Sheared for fullness and shape, with exquisitely long (six inches or fifteen centimetres) needles on branches that curve slightly upward, Scot's pines are showstoppers in the home during the holidays.[22]—SN

CHRISTMAS TREE HOW-TOS

Selecting, Setting Up, and Caring for Your Tree

Since coming to Canada as a child, my family and I have always had a fresh Christmas tree as an essential part of our festivities. From taking the time to select a tree, to putting it up, decorating it, and finally ending the season by taking it down, that tree is woven into the traditions of my family.

But there is a lot more to having a successful Christmas tree than tradition! Right off the bat, it's important to plan a safe location for your tree. Foremostly, that means out of the high traffic areas where the inevitable brushing by and bumping into it and its ornaments will occur. Avoid places with heat vents, fireplaces, radiators, or even a bright window, for that heat will contribute to premature drying of the branches and shorten its time in your home. These days, mine is tucked into a northeast corner where it is always visible as a focal point, but safe from accidents and heat.

Once the decision is made, measure the space. Our eyes are often bigger than the amount of tree the space can handle and coming home with an outsized tree that must be chopped and trimmed to fit is heartbreaking. Include in the measurements the maximum height the tree can be, including a tree topper and the tree stand. As a rule of thumb, allow for at least six inches (fifteen centimetres) clearance between the top of the tree, including the topper, in calculating the tree height. Next, figure out the maximum reach that the branches can have. Also of consideration is the girth of the trunk of the tree. Will it fit into the tree stand? (See p. 50 for more about tree stands). Then step back and visualize if the amount of tree that your heart desires will be in proportion to the space.

Think about the species of tree you should have. We all have our traditional favourites, but others may be a better fit. The space you have may dictate the type of tree that will be best, as some are taller and skinnier and others shorter and fatter. Consider too, how long you want the tree to be in your home. The longer it is to be up, the more needle retention will be a factor in your choice. I often want my tree up for a month at least so I really look at the needle retention qualities of the choices available.

Next is shopping day. Make sure to take your measurements and your handy tape measure, but before you go, get out the tree stand and make sure it is in good repair. Is it large and sturdy enough for the tree you want this year? The larger the tree, the bigger the base of the stand needs to be. The water well also needs to be large enough to hold enough water so that you aren't constantly having it drain dry to the detriment of the tree's longevity.

Bring a blanket or tarp to wrap the tree up before it is placed in, or on top of, your vehicle. And don't forget some heavy gloves.

Should a tree lot be your destination, the trees are often tagged with measurements, but they aren't exact, and usually have a range that is often up to 2 feet (61 centimetres) difference for the same price point. You want one that will be the height you desire to avoid disappointment when you get it home. Ideally the trees should be unwrapped and displayed so you can check for the diameter of the tree trunk and see if the branches are nicely spaced for your ornaments. Many trees in tree lots have been groomed to be bushy and full, but that means that there may not be enough space between branches for ornaments to hang straight. Finally, check to ensure that the trunk is straight.

If the tree lot is heated and the trees are not frozen, then do check the tree for freshness by pulling gently on a twig. Do the needles look dark green and shiny, or dull and yellowing? Do the needles stay on the twig? Do the needles bend into a U shape, indicating lots of internal moisture? Is the twig supple? If yes, these are all signs of a fresh tree. Gently bang the tree to see if lots of needles fall off. There will be some, as needles get damaged in transit and trees naturally shed needles in the inner branches, but there shouldn't be shower of needles. Give it a good sniff. Is that lovely fragrance coming from the tree?

If the tree is still frozen and or wrapped in twine you won't be able to perform these tests but at least check that the colour of the needles is a nice dark green. If you are off to a tree farm or bush, make sure to bring an appropriate saw. Plus, the license to cut a tree if it is on Crown or public land. Indiscriminate cutting of trees in the wild is a big problem that has a detrimental effect on the ecosystem and should be a no-go in the quest for the perfect tree. When cutting down the tree, after assessing the quality much like you would at a tree lot, make sure your cut is at least six inches (fifteen centimetres) below the first branches so that it will fit nicely into the stand.

Transport the tree inside your vehicle, if possible, as it is the safest choice, plus it prevents wind and debris from getting on your lovely tree. To prevent needles and sap from getting onto the vehicle, wrap the tree in the plastic, tarp, or blanket you brought with you. If you must use the top of your vehicle, wrap the tree well and make sure it is very securely tied to the roof. It is important to prevent the tree sliding or becoming free and potentially causing an accident.

Once home, the choice is whether the tree should be put up at once or kept aside for the meantime. If it is to be put up later and the tree is to stay outside, then keep it well wrapped and out of direct sunlight. If it is to be placed in an unheated garage, then store it in a cool corner and keep it wrapped. Do not store the tree in a heated garage.

When the tree is ready to be set up, slice off a bit of trunk to remove the callus that will have formed to seal the cut. Failing to do so will prevent the tree from taking up water. There is no need to remove a large chunk of trunk unless the tree needs to

be sized down despite all your measurements and care. No more than ¼–½ inch (.64–1.25 centimetres) needs to be removed.[23] Sometimes tree lots will cut the base for you and there will be no need to recut the trunk if it is less than six to eight hours between the cut and getting the trunk into water. Ensure that the cut makes for a level base so that it is stable in the tree stand. Avoid diagonal cuts to make the tree stand up straighter, and absolutely do not make a V shaped cut which will make water less available to the tree.

Do not shave off the bark or cambium as this is where the tree will take up most of the water, not the inner heartwood. If you have accidently selected a tree with a trunk too big for your current stand, you need to rush out and get a bigger stand. Damaging the bark at the bottom of the trunk is a surefire way to have your tree dry out fast.

Place the tree in its stand on top of a piece of plastic to protect the floor. If you have pets and children in the home, you can secure the top of the tree to the ceiling or wall as an extra anti-tipping measure. Cats climbing in trees is a great meme, but the results can be dramatic to say the least!

Once up, the tree should always have a substantial amount of water in the well of the tree stand. At first the tree will drink copious amounts of water but after a week the amount will slow down. There is no need for anything other than water, so lose the sugar, bleach, floral preservatives, and other home recipes that are promoted as increasing the longevity of the tree. Avoid hydrogels that absorb water and release it gradually as the tree will drink faster than the gels can release the water and they are dangerous to pets and children. The tree just needs water. There is no need for anti-desiccant sprays which are sometimes applied to needles. Allowing the tree to take up water for as long as it can will make all the difference to how long it lasts in the home. By the way, if the cat or dog likes to drink out of the tree well there is no problem to them or the tree. But you will have to allow for their deprivations and increase the water supply accordingly.

Now you are ready to decorate your tree. I recommend using LED lights as they give off little heat and won't cause the needles to dry out. Suffice it to say, never use lighted candles. It may have been the tradition to place candles in trees before electrical lights were invented but so was burning down the tree and home![24] —JM

Tree Stands

As a rule, a 7-foot (2.1-metre) tree should have a stand with at least a foot (30 centimetres) diameter. If the tree is larger, consider nailing the tree stand to a bigger board for extra footing. A heavily decorated tree tipping over because the stand is too flimsy is a devastating experience. An easy calculation is that for every inch (2.54 centimetre) diameter of trunk, the well should hold 1 quart (4 litres) of water. Make sure the screws or bolts in the stand are heavy duty and long enough to anchor the tree into the stand.

I currently use a heavy steel stand with a 2-foot (61 centimetre) diameter with a well that holds 2 gallons (8 litres) of water for my usual 8-foot (2.43 metre) tree. The anchoring bolts are 4 inches (10 centimetres) long. —JM

Live Christmas Trees

Depending on where you live it might be possible to bring a live tree inside as your festive tree, with the idea that it will be planted outside once the season is over. It is wise to decide if you want to do so ahead of time, so that you can prepare a hole for the tree when the ground isn't frozen. Keep the soil handy in a garage where it won't freeze.

Some points to consider are that these trees are generally bagged and balled with the root ball wrapped in burlap which is then placed in a container with mulch packed around the burlap. The weight of such trees can be upward of 150 pounds (68 kilograms),[25] and the logistics of getting it inside and into an appropriate indoor container can be a challenge. Consider too that you must ensure that the root ball does not dry out at all while it is indoors to avoid root damage. A live tree should be in the home no more than seven to ten days.[26] Once back outside, plant the tree in the prepared hole and mulch in well. After spending time in your heated home, the tree will have started to come out of dormancy and may not survive the transition to the garden. At the very least, it may suffer transplant shock and will require especially attentive care come spring to settle into the garden. —JM

Recycling Your Christmas Tree

You know it is time to take down your tree when the fragrance becomes stronger as the needles dry out. It is a sad day for my family when it is time to say goodbye to our tree, but we take solace in knowing that it will stay in our garden in one form or another for perpetuity.

Allow the water level in the tree well to drop, so that there won't be a lot of spillage when lifting the tree out. Have a tree bag or big tarp handy to place the tree on once it is free from the stand. Wrap the tree up carefully to prevent shedding needles from getting in the home, and take it outside.

Many municipalities have arrangements to dispose of trees after the festivities are over. The trees are put to good use by being mulched for city parks. But keeping that tree at home is even better. In my home, I start by plunking the tree in a snowbank and decorating it with DIY bird feeders made from pinecones and suet to attract the birds. Squirrels love to run off with the cones, too.

After a while, I chop off branches to lay down over perennials to protect them and keep the soil frozen as the early spring sun melts the snow. Some boughs can be arranged to provide shelter for birds and mammals.

Come late spring the rest of the branches are chopped off and the ones being used for cover are lifted. They are placed in a pile in a corner of the garden to provide summer shelter and habitat for wildlife. The trunk can be used as a support for plants. I always have a couple of trunks from previous years handy and they make a great tripod.

Finally in the fall, that trunk gets used to make wood cookies for ornaments. That tree just keeps on giving! —JM

THE GREENS USED IN WREATHS, OUTDOOR ARRANGEMENTS, GARLANDS, AND INDOOR ARRANGEMENTS

There are so many greens that can be used to create wreaths, outdoor arrangements, garlands, and indoor arrangements. They can be foraged from native plants in your area, harvested from your garden, or purchased from a tree lot or greenhouse. Many trimmings or branches from species used as Christmas trees are perfect to create your choice of decoration. Being evergreen is the greatest attribute a plant used as decoration can have. Besides those species already mentioned as being perfect for the Christmas tree, here are more species that are often used at this time of year.

Boxwood and Oregonia

Box or boxwood (*Buxus sempervirens*) is a broadleaf evergreen shrub in the Buxaceae family. These are slow growing shrubs that are native to the southern portions of Europe, Asia, and the Americas. Most species are not hardy enough to survive the winters in northern climes, though a few cultivars such as 'Green Mountain' or 'Green Gem' are proving to be hardy as winter moderates in Canada. I have three growing in my Calgary garden, though I seldom pinch any branches for my arrangements as I value them so much in the landscape.

Boxwood is known for its small, dark green, leathery, and round leaves that are held oppositely on slender branches. Those branches are marvelous in all manner of arrangements, both for inside and outside the home, and retain their leaves in spite of the temperature, which is usually freezing outside and warm inside.

Oregonia (*B. sempervirens* 'Variegata') is a beautiful cultivar of boxwood that features small, creamy white and green variegated leaves held stiffly on sturdy branches. It is also a great performer in all arrangements.[27] —JM

Cedar

Many species are known as cedar, from the cedars of Lebanon (*Cedrus libani*) to the eastern red cedar or Virginia juniper (*Juniperus virginiana*), as well as the western red cedar (*Thuja plicata*) and eastern white cedar (*Thuja occidentalis*), native to western and eastern Canada respectively..

Cedar is often called *arbor vitae* or "tree of life"[28] for its manifold uses in housing, transportation, clothing, tools, medicines, teas, and more. It was used as a tea to cure the scurvy that Jacques Cartier's men suffered from in the sixteenth century.[29]

Cedar (*Thuja* spp.) is part of the Cupressaceae family. The western red cedar can be a magnificent 200 foot (60 metre) tall tree in a pyramidal shape. Eastern white cedar is slower growing and may only reach 65 feet (20 metres) tall. Horizontal to drooping branches have branchlets with sprays of tiny, flat, scale-like leaves that are bright green on top and a dark waxy green on the bottom.

Cedar is one of the major greens used for making outdoor arrangements, garlands, wreaths, and indoor arrangements. Typically, western red cedar is used in the western half of Canada and America while eastern white cedar is common in the eastern half of the continent.

The graceful droopy branchlets can be easily woven into wreaths and garlands either by themselves or together with other greens. The branches lend themselves beautifully to outdoor arrangements as well indoor arrangements. Cedar has terrific foliage retention, as well as keeping its suppleness and colour, and takes a long time to dry out. The fragrance of the foliage is long lasting, making it desirable to include bits of cedar in recipes for potpourri too.

Incense cedar (*Calocedrus decurrens*) is not a true cedar, though it is also part of Cupressaceae. Its foliage greatly resembles that of species in *Thuja*, though is lighter green and distinguished by scent nodules at the ends of the leaves. It gives off a strong aroma when the foliage is crushed that some liken to the smell of shoe polish. Typically incense cedar is used in indoor arrangements where the fragrance of its branches can be appreciated and is often an accent green rather than structural green.[30] —JM

Eucalyptus

Eucalyptus is a genus of some 700 species, mostly native to Australia, in the myrtle family, Myrtaceae. They can be trees or shrubs, and nearly all are evergreen in their native habitat, where they are commonly known as gum trees.

Mature leaves are a glossy or waxy blue-green, lanceolate in shape. Those of immature plants, often used in arrangements or wreaths, are rounded and glaucous, leading them to be called "silver dollar." Both mature and immature leaves have a strong fragrance due to the oil glands that cover their surfaces. The oil produced from the leaves has many medicinal benefits.

What makes eucalyptus appealing as a green for seasonal arrangements is their longevity, retaining both colour, form, and fragrance for many weeks. Not to mention, they have a unique form among greens and are used both in fresh, dried, and seasonal arrangements to great effect.[31] —JM

Grapevines

There are an estimated twenty-five species of grapes (*Vitus* spp.) native to North America, and countless other varieties that are grown for fresh eating, wine, juice, preserves, and other products. A fun holiday tradition in Spain called "Las doce uvas de la suerte," or The Twelve Lucky Grapes, has participants indulge in eating twelve green grapes for every second the clock strikes at midnight leading into the new year. Success means that fortune will follow, but it truly sounds like a difficult eating challenge, especially if the grapes are not seedless!

In addition to delicious, versatile fruit, grapes also supply woody vines that are ideal for bending into wreaths. Grapevines should be cut while the plants are dormant, in late autumn through early winter. Vines that are green instead of dried and brown are much easier to work with, and of course, you'll want to keep a few of those lovely decorative tendrils in place. Work with vines that are about 7–8 feet (2.1 to 2.4 metres) long to give you sufficient material to play with—you can always cut away excess with a pair of secateurs.[32]—SN

Magnolia

In the southern United States, magnolia trees are at their most resplendent in the spring, when their magnificent show-stopping blooms burst forth with a highly appealing sweet fragrance. There are over 300 magnolia species native to parts of southern and eastern China as well as many parts of the United States (as well as one small-sized species, *M. acuminata*, endemic to Ontario, Canada). Of course, the timeline is wrong for using magnolia flowers for holiday arrangements; it's the lovely wide evergreen leaves of southern magnolia, *M. grandiflora*, that are valued for wreath-making. Dark green on one side, with a fuzzy copper-coloured underside, magnolia leaves can be used either fresh or dried (the leaves will pale beautifully with age). Collected in the fall, the unusual cone-like seedpods of *M. grandiflora* are worth drying and twisting into wreaths as decorations guaranteed to spark curiosity.[33]—SN

Noble Fir

The noble fir (*Abies procera*), also known as the red fir or simply Christmas tree, is truly a noble tree. Native to the Pacific coastal ranges of northern California, Oregon, and Washington, a mature tree can easily grow some 200 feet (61 metres) and is the largest of the firs. It features stiff 1-inch (2.54-centimetre) blue-green needles that go around the twigs like a spruce but are twisted upward so that the bottom of the twig is exposed and shows off the needles' silver-white undersides.

Grown as a Christmas tree, and sometimes called the "King of Christmas Trees,"[34] they have a strong conical form, with well-spaced, stiff branches that are more than capable of holding up the heaviest of ornaments.[35] Noble fir retains its needles extremely well, making the tree a long-lasting feature of the season. The rich fragrance lasts and lasts, too.

Noble fir branches readily lend themselves to being used for other seasonal greenery. As the main branch for a swag, they are stellar, with their sturdy form being the perfect foil for other types of greens. As a garland, the smaller bits of the branches can be readily woven into the strand, adding considerable texture and form. The longevity of the needles really makes the noble fir a standout as a single species garland or together with other greens. The ability to keep going without additional water is a definite plus. Likewise, with wreaths, especially bare twig wreaths, the stiff nature of the twigs and needles can be an asset.

In outdoor containers, noble fir can form part of the upright framework, though it's very stiff nature can be a drawback if attempting to use the green for filling in the centre of the arrangement, and it positively resists being used to spill over the edges of the container and droop gracefully. Rather, it sticks straight out, so other greens are necessary to provide the desired effect.

I seldom, if ever, use noble fir for indoor arrangements. In these often smaller arrangements the stiff nature of noble fir can be a real drawback. But that is no problem as there are other fir species ready to take up the slack.[35] —JM

Salal

Salal (*Gaultheria shallon*) is a dense understory evergreen shrub native to the Pacific Northwest of the United States and Canada, that is in the heath or heather family, Ericaceae. Known as salal in North America, it is also called *shallon*. In England, where it is an introduced plant and now considered an invasive species, it is known as *gaultheria*. It features large dark green leaves that are glossy and leathery with pointed tips.

Salal branches and leaves are used extensively in floral arrangements, where they are often referred to as salal lemon leaves. The stems are long-lasting in fresh and dried arrangements alike, and a perfect foil or filler for bouquets and set pieces.

Where salal also shines is in seasonal greens arrangements, notably for outside arrangements such as wreaths or large containers. The leaves take very well to being exposed to freezing temperatures and will not turn black after been frozen. As an accent green, salal is a staple for professional florists and home decorators alike.[36] —JM

Silver Fir

European silver fir (*Abies alba*) is not the same species you'll find in North America, where the Pacific silver fir (*Abies amabilis*) is distributed along the coastal regions of the Pacific Northwest. European silver fir, found across the mountainous regions of Europe, is famous for taking centre stage in the gloomy holiday cautionary tale "The Little Fir Tree" by Hans Christian Andersen. Much more cheerfully, both European silver fir and Pacific silver fir have stiff boughs ideal for working into wreaths. The green foliage with silver undersides is highly attractive, and the needles don't drop readily.[37]—SN

White Pine

North American native Eastern white pine (*Pinus strobus*) has massive historical significance as its great height (200 feet or 60 metres) made it highly suitable for building masts for ships in the seventeenth and eighteenth centuries. When an introduced pathogen, white pine blister rust, threatened the timber industry, governments in both the United States and Canada were quick to prohibit the cultivation of currants and gooseberries, which were alternate hosts of the pathogen. This ban was in full effect from the 1920s to the 1960s, and still exists in some states today. (There are now disease-resistant cultivars of *Ribes* spp. as well as white pines available.)

Eastern white pine is highly desirable in wreath-making due to its luxuriously soft, feathery light blue-green needles that are borne on the stems in clusters of five. The needles can reach a length of up to five inches (twelve centimetres). If you can find a bough with cones, you're in for an additional treat as the cones are cylindrical and large, up to eight inches (twenty centimetres) long.[38]—SN

WREATHS

Symbolism

Wreaths, those simple circles of greenery, have a wealth of symbolism and use throughout the ages. They represent the circle of life, immortality, renewal, and rejuvenation. They also represent wisdom, power, authority, and honour among many other qualities.

Originally wreaths were placed on heads, necks, and arms, not our walls. There is a legend that long ago a magician created a wreath out of leaves and placed it over his head so it rested on his ears and allowed him to hear the secrets of trees.[39] Thus, wreaths have long been associated with magical powers.

Legend or not, the ancient Persians, Egyptians, Greeks, and Romans created laurel wreaths as symbols of honour and victory. They were worn by priests, athletes, brides, and noble guests. In the festival of Saturnalia, among the many festivals at the winter solstice, wreaths were symbols of renewal as the cycle of the seasons turned. In ancient Nordic and Germanic cultures, wreaths were part of Yule and were symbols of spring bringing forth a renewal of life.

Wreaths as part of the Christmas festival have their origins in the fifteenth century in Britain and Europe. They were created from evergreen boughs and twisted to form circles that adorned people's homes. Often the evergreens came from the trimmings left over from shaping the Christmas tree into a triangle. The word *wreath* is derived from the Old English *writhian* meaning "twisted."[40] As wreaths became more and more a part of Christmas traditions, they came to signify the love of God, which has no beginning or end.[41]

By the nineteenth century, the custom of laying a wreath flat on a table and setting candles in it to represent the weeks of

Advent came about, with a new candle lit as each week passed. In the centre was the Christ candle, lit on Christmas Day. These days many wreaths adorn our doors and walls, decorated with berries, pinecones, fruit, and more, and if hung on the front door, serve as a hospitable welcome to the home. —JM

Types of Wreath Frames

There are so many kinds of wreaths ranging from simple to very elaborate. When it comes to making an evergreen wreath, there are a few options for the frame upon which bundles of evergreen foliage are secured.

Bare Twig

A wreath can be as straightforward as cutting withes (young branches) of willow or dogwood, then bending them into a circle and binding them together. You can make them easily, and they can be as thick as you wish according to the number of withes you use. I have done them with as few as two stems and as thick as six, though the more stems you use the more you seem to need a third hand to manage the process. Having a friend help with the binding is a Godsend!

A sturdier wreath can be made from grape vines that are once again twisted and woven into a circle and bound together for strength. You can make these yourself or purchase them pre-made. Likewise, rattan or wicker wreath forms can be purchased already made.

A bare twig wreath has the considerable benefit of being reusable year after year. Once the season is over, the decorations and foliage can be removed and the frame can be used to make other seasonal wreaths. Foliage fixed to the frame will dry out fairly quickly, especially on wreaths that are inside, as there is no means of providing moisture to the attached greens. —JM

Wire Frames

A wreath can also be made using a wire frame composed of three to five rounds of wire, held together with cross braces, often with a shallow well to make it easy to layer in decorative materials. These frames come in multiple diameters and shapes. Some of them have *teeth,* short U-shaped wires sticking up from the base to help hold the materials on the frame.

There are three main ways to build up the wreath frame. When using evergreen boughs, the simplest way is to bind bunches of greens directly to the wire frame. Alternatively, one can pack moistened straw into the frame, binding it in with tie wire. The resulting wreath can either be decorated as is or used to further bind evergreen and broadleaf greens. Lastly, one can make a moss wreath by packing pre-moistened sphagnum moss onto the frame and binding it into place similarly to that of a straw base, with bundles of greens then affixed to the moss.

Wire frames can be disassembled after the season by cutting the securing wires and removing the decorations and foliage so that the frames reused. Should the greens be bound onto the frame without a base, they will dry out as quickly as those attached to a bare twig wreath. A straw or mossed wreath has the advantage of providing a source of moisture for the greens, and generally these wreaths will last longer. —JM

How to Make a Wreath

Regardless of the type of wreath base you use, there is a straightforward technique for creating your wreath. Start by laying your frame on a flat surface. Attach a spool of 22-gauge floral wire to one of the cross sections of your wire frame or to a sturdy twig if you are using a bare twig frame.

Then cut pieces of all the greens you are going to use and place them in piles for handy access. The pieces should be between six and eight inches (fifteen and twenty centimetres) as a rule, as longer pieces are hard to work with and secure properly to the frame.

Create a bundle of greens with three or four pieces, lay it on the frame, and secure it by tightly wrapping the floral wire over the stems. Lay a second bundle beside the first but further along the frame, so that there is an overlap of foliage to hide the stems and wire of the first bundle. Continue around the frame until you reach the starting point with the last bundle hiding the stems and wire of that first bundle. If you are happy with the arrangement of bundles and the entire frame is hidden by the foliage, then tie off the wire by looping it through the base and threading it back onto a support or twig so the wire cannot loosen.

If the entire wreath is not to be covered with foliage, then the first bundle of greens will need to be tucked into the base so that the stems and wire are not seen, and the last bundle will need to have its stems tucked through the foliage of the second last bundle to avoid them being exposed. Floral pins help with securing the stems neatly.

Hold the wreath up to make sure that all the pieces are nicely secured. If any are floppy or seeming a bit loose, then secure them to the frame individually with floral pins. Spray the foliage with a floral hydrating spray, coating the greens with a botanical oil which will prevent the foliage from drying out too quickly. Now you are ready to decorate your wreath![42] —JM

Decorating Wreaths

Wreaths are traditionally decorated simply with bows, cones, and berries, though birds, fruit, and other decorations can be added to suit the theme of the wreath. Bows can be tied to the wreath with wire. Other decorations can be made into picks by inserting a skewer into the object and, if need be, held in place with hot glue. Then the pick is simply pushed into the wreath with the foliage hiding the wooden skewer. —JM

GARLANDS

A garland is a chain or band of vines, flowers, and leaves that is used to decorate our homes in times of celebration.[43] A small garland can be made into a circle and placed on statutes or people, similarly to wreaths. Garlands have been used since ancient times, from funeral ceremonies, where the departed wore them, to victory celebrations, and are woven throughout religious life in many cultures.

Garlands came into their own for Christmas celebrations during Victorian times in England, where the custom of lavishly decorating our homes came to the forefront. While the Christmas tree was the focal point, a garland was the unifier with loops of greens hung on walls, around doorways, and across beams.[44] While foliage garlands prevailed, signifying family unity and traditions, other garlands came into being. Whether it is a simple paper chain garland made by children, the cranberry and popcorn garland that evolved in North America, strings of candies and fruit, or the tinsel prevalent these days, garlands are interwoven into the celebrations of the season. —JM

Making a Foliage Garland

The key to making an evergreen foliage garland is organization! You will need:

- A flat surface to work on as well as a means to clamp or tie off the growing garland. It can be a C-clamp or a chair leg for that matter.
- A length of rope, twine, or wire that is as long as you need the garland to be. Or several shorter lengths that can be joined together once the sections are made if it is to be a long garland. I prefer green rustic wire, which is wire with twine wrapped around it, as it is sturdy yet flexible.
- 22- or 24-gauge floral wire, pre-cut into 4–6 inch (10–15 centimetre) lengths.
- Piles of foliage that have been pre-cut into bits that range from 6–12 inches (15–30 centimetres) long depending on the look that you want for the garland.
- Pruners, needle nose pliers, and gloves.

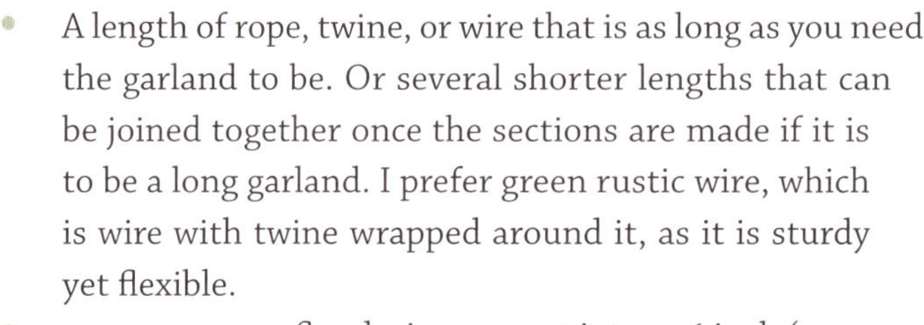

To make the garland, take small bundles of greens and tie them tightly together with the floral wire, using the needle nose pliers to really make the wire tight. The stems will shrink as they dry, and you don't want them slipping out. Then attach the bundle to the rope, twine, or wire with the ends of the floral wire. Use the pliers again to twist the wire tightly so that it is snugged up against the main length. Then tie another bundle together and lay it down with some overlapping the first bundle so that the stems and wire are hidden. Continue down the length of the rope, twine, or wire until you reach the end, then tie in a smaller bundle to finish off the garland, tucking in the ends of the twigs. Do make sure to leave at least a foot (thirty centimetres) of the garland bare so that you can tie it nicely to posts or banister spindles. You can also make loops at the end to hang it off hooks mounted on walls and so forth.

Then comes the fun of decorating, with your favourite accents being wired onto the garland. Most garlands are either left undecorated or simply decorated with natural materials such as cones and berries. But really, the sky is the limit for what you chose to add to your garland.

Once completed, your garland will not have access to moisture to keep the foliage fresh. Do choose the freshest materials you can find, and it possible, place the branches in a bucket of water to soak up moisture beforehand. For added moisture, you can either mist the garland with water or use a floral spray before decorating. If your garland is to be outside, and if you live in a region that is cold throughout the celebrations, then it will last up to eight weeks or so. Inside, in central heating, misting the garland every so often with help keep it fresh. Avoid placing your garland close to a heat source (I really don't recommend over the mantel if it is a real fireplace!). Most garland indoors will last nicely for a month.[45] —JM

OUTDOOR ARRANGEMENTS

Making your own outdoor arrangement to adorn your front step, or anywhere in your garden for that matter, is an immensely satisfying and creative way to celebrate the season. Creating that outdoor arrangement requires technique, equipment, plus your creativity and enthusiasm.

Outdoor arrangements can be in any container that you have on hand or wish to purchase. Containers range from urns to oak barrels, tin containers, ceramic pots, and more. I often use mâché pots made from recycled cardboard as either a stand-alone container or as an insert into a larger container. I also line the container with a plastic bag so that it will hold moisture in the soil, sand, or floral oasis used to hold the stems in place, though that step is not necessary if you are making an arrangement directly into an outdoor container with existing soil. A lot will depend on whether you live in an area where the soil will already be frozen when it comes time to make your arrangement. Where I live in Calgary, it is the norm for that soil to be frozen solid by December, so I prepare outdoor containers ahead of time by scooping out the soil to the depth of the pot I am using as an insert, then mound moistened mulch around it to keep it in place once I pop in the arrangement. If your soil is not frozen then you can use the existing growing media and insert boughs directly into it. Just be sure to water the media after the boughs are in so that they are properly anchored.

Assemble the foliage that you will be using, whether it is boughs foraged from your garden, those from the wild where you have obtained a license to cut, or material purchased from a nursery. Be aware that some species of evergreen trees and shrubs such as spruce or juniper are very stiff and not as easy to work with as others, such as cedar, white pine, or fir. Consider adding in a specialty green or two that will tolerate being frozen and not

turn black. Magnolia, salal, incense cedar, eucalyptus, boxwood, and oregonia are just a few of the choices available at local nurseries. Snip off a bit of the stem from each bough and place them in a bucket of water for a few hours ahead of making the arrangement so that the branches can uptake some of the water. I leave my foliage in the buckets overnight before I assemble my arrangements.

Consider if you will be using permanent botanical accents in the arrangement such as birch logs, dogwood, or other interesting twigs, berries (real or artificial), pinecones, and seed pods, as they will be an integral part of the design.

Now you are ready to create your arrangement. I often use the cardinal principal of design, that of having elements of thriller, spiller, and filler. The thriller is the bold, vertical, eye-catching part of the arrangement. The spillers are the boughs that flow over the side of the container adding flow to the design. The fillers are the boughs in the middle, surrounding the thriller and filling in the arrangement.

You can start by inserting the thriller boughs, then stepping it down to create the filler layer, and then finish off the arrangement with the spillers which will gracefully flow over the sides of the container. Or you can start by creating that spiller layer and build it up from there. I often find that it is the boughs themselves that seem to direct my technique as you need to work with each one to place it where it will be seen to the greatest effect. Most boughs have a mind of their own, so you need to work with their natural curvature and drape as you create the arrangement. It is tempting to keep stuffing in more and more boughs until the arrangement is very full. However, an arrangement can be too full, preventing you from seeing the individual boughs due to the forest that has been created. Over the years, I have found I use less foliage but to greater effect. You want to see the beauty of each bough, not a general mass of foliage.

At this point, I spray the boughs with a botanical spray that is designed to coat the foliage and both hydrate and prevent it from drying out too quickly in the sun and wind. In Calgary, this added step is necessary because of our Chinook winds, which periodically thaw the arrangement and dry it out.

Once you are happy with the foliage, insert your botanical accents to their best advantage. Often the bigger elements can serve as the thriller or provide focal points in the arrangement. Step back once you are done and consider the whole arrangement. Does it seem to be in balance, with each element unifying to create a satisfying whole? Or are there elements that are out of sync? Now is the time to adjust anything out of place.

Next is adding in accessories such as bows, ornaments, and any other favourite piece that is a tradition to have in your container. Mine is a plaid felt moose I acquired years ago. I have even included a small bird house on occasion, as well as rattan animals on picks. The sky is the limit. But don't go overboard with the decorations. Simplicity allows for each one to shine, and if you have more that you have accumulated over the years, you can always build another arrangement!

Once the arrangement has been made and is outside, it will freeze in place if you are in a region that stays below the freezing mark through the season. There is literally nothing to do but enjoy it. Should you live where temperatures are highly variable or always stay above the freezing mark, then you will need to ensure that the medium the arrangement is in stays moist. You can add a jug of water every so often as the medium dries out, as those boughs will continue to uptake water for at least the first couple of weeks. The more water they take up the longer the arrangement will stay fresh.

Once the season is over, I often remove some of the more festive decorations and continue to enjoy the simple beauty of the arrangement until it loses its green colour as the warming sun bleaches and dries out the boughs come spring. —JM

INDOOR ARRANGEMENTS

Beside creating arrangements for outside the home, there are a whole range of possibilities for creating indoor arrangements with seasonal greens decorated to one's taste.

Containers should be spill-proof as you don't want water damaging furniture or floors. Purpose made containers of plastic, china, tin, or wood with a plastic insert to keep water inside are most appropriate. So are vases, cookie jars or tins, teapots, and coffee mugs. Literally any container can be used to great effect to create an indoor foliage arrangement.

Before starting, visualize the size and shape of the finished arrangement. If you are making a centerpiece for the dining room table, with or without a candle, it should be low enough for people to see over it while seated. It should also be in proportion to the size of the table and not so large that it takes necessary space away from dishes.[46] If the arrangement is meant for a side table, buffet, or desk then ensure it will be of an appropriate size to be effective; not too small or too big.

Start by filling your container with premoistened floral foam or tangled wire so you can carefully insert the foliage. As with outdoor arrangements, foliage should be placed so that it spills over the sides of the container, then a filler layer should be added, and if appropriate, a thriller to draw the eye. Once foliage is well placed, spray the arrangement with a floral spray to hydrate the foliage and protect it from drying out.

Decorate with cones, berries, and other favourite ornaments and place in your desired location, hopefully away from hot air vents, radiators, or fireplaces.

The foliage will draw up water from the container at a great rate for the first week, so be sure to fill the container with water periodically. If cared for, indoor arrangements can easily last for six weeks or more. —JM

Chapter 3.

HOUSEPLANTS to CELEBRATE the SEASON

There are so many plants grown for the home in this special season. While a few are associated with the holidays because their bloom time matches this time of year, most have deeper meanings and symbolism attached to them. Many are native to warmer climates where they can be outdoors or inside. Some may be considered weeds or are hard to control where they grow naturally. (Janet is thinking of the huge poinsettia shrub in the garden of her childhood, which was macheted down to the ground every few months!)

In colder areas of the world, they adorn our homes, some blooming and lasting just a few weeks. Others become part of the year-round collection of plants and delight us when the time to come out of dormancy and bloom is upon us once again.

THE PLANTS

AMARYLLIS
Standing Tall and Proud

There exists much confusion about amaryllis. The genus *Amaryllis* is native to South Africa and consists of just two species, one of which is *Amaryllis belladonna*, also called the belladonna lily, as they greatly resemble lilies in the size and shape of their flowers.

The bulbs that we commonly call amaryllis are generally hybrid cultivars of the genus *Hippeastrum* of which there are some ninety species that are native to tropical and subtropical areas of the Americas. Both genera are part of the Amaryllidaceae family, which could account for the confusion. Regardless of the botany behind it all, we know these bulbs as amaryllis, and amaryllis they will remain to us. Prized for their gorgeous, outsized blooms in deepest red through brilliant white and strappy dark green leaves, they bloom when there are few other flowers blooming, lifting our spirits and contributing to the festivities.

The choice of bulbs can be a perennial favourite like 'Red Lion,' through to one of my favourites, 'Picotee' onwards to the reindeer series with 'Rudolph, 'Donner,' 'Blitzen,' and so on. It seems like there are new varieties to try each year.

Growing amaryllis can quickly become a passion, perhaps even an addiction, and I know of gardeners with upward of twenty in their homes. I try to keep my collection down to a reasonable six or so, but it is with great excitement that I await the bulbs' arrival in garden centres come late fall so I can select a new one for the season.

The bulbs come either bare root or already potted, but in either case, try to get the largest bulb you can find and afford. The bigger the bulb, the more stems will grow from it, upward of three or even four for the largest ones. Look for bulbs that are firm and intact with no wounds or mould. For preference, they should still be in a dormant state, though it is common to see flower stalks already starting to emerge from the top of the bulb. Avoid bulbs that are seriously growing already as they will be stressed.

Once home, select a narrow pot that has good drainage and is heavy enough that it won't tip over when the plant is blooming. It should be about two inches (five centimetres) wider than the diameter of the bulb as these bulbs like to be pot-bound, and deep enough for good root development to occur. Fill the pot two-thirds full of fresh potting soil, then place the bulb on top and backfill more soil around the bulb. The bulb should not be totally buried, but rather sit perched on the soil with perhaps just the bottom half buried underneath. The roots are going to firmly anchor the plant once it starts growing and blooming.

Water thoroughly and place in bright, indirect light. These bulbs are primed and ready to grow, and very quickly you will see leaves and flower stalks growing. Do water whenever the top couple of inches (five centimetres) of soil is dry and use a half-strength liquid fertilizer every time you water to promote flower development.

You can expect the bulbs to be blooming in about a month to six weeks, with flowers lasting a week to ten days depending on how hot your home is generally. Remove the flower stalk after it finishes blooming as you do not want the plant to direct energy to seed formation. Allow the leaves to yellow and die back before snipping them off. But continue to water the plant, and come spring, take it outside in a part-shade, part-sun location to continue growing and storing up energy for further blooming.

If you want to control when your amaryllis will rebloom—as in, during the winter months—then come late summer, bring them inside and store them in a cool, dark closet. Do not water them during this time, and as the leaves dry, cut them off. After

eight to twelve weeks, bring them out of the dark, water and fertilize as before, and set them in a sunny window. Soon they will start to send up a flower stalk and leaves, and you are going to have another lovely show for the season.[46] —JM

CHRISTMAS CACTUS
Hope and Resilience

The Christmas cactus does not at first glance appear to be a plant associated with the cold and dark of Northern Hemisphere winter celebrations. Originating in the coastal forests of Brazil, this tropical plant in the Cactaceae family seems an oddity indeed. Yet any plant that blooms in the winter months is welcomed and absorbed into the festivities!

There is a legend that a Jesuit missionary, Father Jose, was given Christmas cactus blooms by children in a village as a sign of his acceptance.[47] Certainly the symbolism of this joyfully blooming plant is that of faith, community, and the spirit of giving that is associated with the celebrations of this time of year.

Named for the time of year it blooms, Christmas cactus is part of the small *Schlumbergera* genus, and the original Christmas cactus may well have been *S. bridgesii*. This species, as well as *S. russelliana,* have been bred with *S. truncata* to form the Buckleyi group (*S.* × *buckleyi*) of cultivars that typically bloom toward the end of the year. Another group, that of Truncata, tend to bloom earlier in the year and are often called Easter cactus or Thanksgiving cactus as a result, though sometimes things get mixed up and blooms occur off season.

Members of *Schlumbergera* do not look like the prickly species that we commonly associate with cactus. Plants are often six to twelve inches (fifteen to thirty centimetres) tall but can spread up to two or three feet (sixty to ninety centimetres) depending on the age of the plants. They have soft, flat, modified stem segments joined together, commonly thought to be the leaves, which can droop over the sides of the pot. Flower buds emerge from areoles found at terminal segment and occasionally from the sides of lower segments. The tubular flowers face downward with upward of twenty or so tepals, in colours ranging from red, through pink and orange to white. Each bloom lasts but a few days, but a plant in full bloom is a colourful sight.

As a cactus, what these plants want is bright indirect light. Do allow the soil to completely dry out before watering thoroughly. They prefer temperatures around 70 to 80° F (21 to 27° C) throughout the growing season. Do fertilize with a diluted solution in spring and early summer to promote growth. They also like to be in the same spot, so don't bother turning them around to face a different direction.

Christmas cactus has a reputation for being finickity when it comes reblooming. What should be understood is that the cactus has a thermo-photoperiodic response to different conditions that triggers buds forming and blooms opening. To trigger this response, come September provide 13–15 uninterrupted hours of night and cooler temperatures in the range of 55 to 65° F (13 to 18° C). You will soon see those buds forming and can cheer the upcoming flourish of blooms. Remember to keep the soil moist but not wet after buds form to prevent them aborting.

Having said that, I often neglect to provide these conditions, but somehow the plant manages on its own, developing buds anyway and providing a show regardless of my inattention. Once that happens, do not move or otherwise change the conditions the plant is growing in, or flower buds may drop. Which means that when we buy Christmas cactus from a store come the festive season, they often lose their buds and flowers to our dismay. Better to buy a plant earlier in the year, get it used to its new growing conditions, and provide the conditions to trigger bud growth come the fall.

Once you have figured out what your particular Christmas cactus wants from you to be healthy, it will last for years, even decades, and reward you every year with a fantastic show of blooms at just the right time to be part of the festive season.[48] —JM

CYCLAMEN
Terrific Tubers

The truly special tropical-looking blooms of *Cyclamen persicum* (known as the florist's cyclamen) will have everyone gaping (and possibly gasping) at their beauty; this is one plant that is guaranteed to spark admiration. Abundant colourful blooms in red, orange, white, purple, and pink rise on thin stems above compact marbled green foliage. Some cultivars have ruffled double blooms. *C. persicum* is considered a houseplant and grown indoors in pots in most parts of the world, but there are other species, such as *C. hederifolium* that are grown outdoors in climates that closely mimic the plant's native distribution in the Mediterranean. When grown indoors, the plant needs bright, indirect light during its growing season, which begins in the autumn. Through the summer, the plant is largely dormant and will not require much light (and you'll want to withhold the fertilizer and go easy on watering during this time as well). The plant will become a bit scraggly and possibly lose some of its leaves during dormancy, but it will rebound in the fall and be downright spectacular by the time midwinter—and all its celebrations—arrive.

Cyclamen has very specific needs that must be met to keep it happy, so when you bring it home from the grocery store or garden centre, be aware that it is not good with too much heat or any chilly drafts. If you can keep it in an area of your home where the nighttime temperature hovers around 50° F (10° C) that would be ideal. When you water, do so from the base so that you don't glug liquid into the crown or on the leaves of the plant; this encourages rot.

Cyclamen grows from tubers, so it's best to divide them when you wish to propagate your plant. Cuttings are rarely successful and seeds for most of the varieties we have available as gardeners are sterile.

Besides the fact that cyclamen bloom around the holiday season—and do it extremely well—there is another, albeit a bit vague, connection to Judeo-Christian beliefs. In the Song of Solomon found in the Hebrew Bible, there are references to several plants in the garden of Gethsemane, including rose of sharon and lily of the valley. It is thought that cyclamen may be one of the plants grouped in with these others, as it would have been growing in the region at the time.[49]—SN

KALANCHOE
Bringing the Tropics into Your Home for the Holidays

There are more than one hundred species of *Kalanchoe* worldwide and many of them are suitable for use as houseplants, but the one that most people associate with the holiday season is *K. blossfeldiana*. The common name is flaming katy or widow's thrill, and when it blooms, it's a thrill, indeed! Native to Madagascar and distributed through several sub-tropical and tropical regions, kalanchoe has gorgeous bright clusters of blooms with bold colours: yellow, red, orange, pink, and coral. In North America, it is common to find kalanchoe in full flower and ready for the holiday table at most garden centres and even in supermarkets during the Christmas season. Rich green, shiny, succulent leaves complement the blooms and bring an "evergreen" look to the home.

Once the holiday season has ended and the flowers have faded, kalanchoe makes an easy-care houseplant. It grows slowly, but its two big requirements are simple to fulfill: don't overwater it, and ensure it has enough bright, indirect sunlight. Offer your plant a balanced fertilizer once a year, in the spring, and simply enjoy the beautiful foliage and attractive mounding shape. Kalanchoe will rebloom if it is happy, which usually occurs when you've obeyed the two rules on a consistent basis, and the plant

has been exposed to the appropriate photoperiod. Be aware that this is another plant you don't want to expose your pets to due to its toxicity.[50]—SN

NORFOLK ISLAND PINE
The Living Christmas Tree

Around the holiday season, garden centres and big box stores are packed with displays of potted evergreens with graceful, long branches and short, soft needles that curve inward. They may come decorated with bows and bells. These are Norfolk Island pines, and despite their appearance, they are not at all accustomed to cold climates. Ensure they are wrapped up for that trip to the car from the store!

Originating in New Zealand, Norfolk Island pine (*Araucaria heterophylla*) isn't a pine at all; it's actually related to monkey puzzle tree, an evergreen native to Chile and Argentina. In the wild, Norfolk Island pine can grow to a whopping 200 feet (60 metres) tall, but you'll be incredibly fortunate if it hits 8 feet (2.4 metres) in your home. (And they grow so slowly it would take years for it to get there.)

In sub-tropical locations in the United States and other parts of the world, Norfolk Island pines may be grown outdoors, where they thrive in direct sunlight. They require regular, consistent watering and soil with a slightly acidic pH (4.5–5.5) but are otherwise low-maintenance and very long-lived.

If you live on the Canadian prairies like me, your Norfolk Island pine will be a large houseplant year-round, with an annual stint at playing Christmas tree. Getting enough light is a big deal for this plant; the branches will begin to droop or even stretch if the light is too low. If you've met the plant's craving for plenty of light, the only other thing you really must think about, besides regular watering, is offering a balanced fertilizer sparingly from spring through autumn. Norfolk Island pine like their growing medium to be a bit lean; overfertilizing will cause leggy growth and a buildup of salts in the potting mix, which can cause the plant to have difficulty taking up water.

One final care tip for your indoor Norfolk Island pine: in our dry central-heated homes, the needles can desiccate during the winter months. Combat this by giving the plant a shower every couple of weeks—the extra humidity will be welcome.[51]—SN

PAPERWHITES
Bulbs for Happiness

Sunny yellow daffodils are a sight for sore eyes in the spring, but I may love paperwhites—their *Narcissus* relatives—even more as they brighten up a room in winter. A lovely wicker basket holding a bunch of blooming paperwhite bulbs can't be beat as a gift for friends and family or placed as a simple decoration on the mantel. Not only are they beautiful, but paperwhites have a strong, sweet fragrance that adds to their appeal.

Paperwhites originate in the Mediterranean and Central Asia, and they were likely brought to China one thousand years ago by traders from Arabia. It took until the nineteenth century for the bulbs to gain popularity in western Europe, particularly in the Netherlands, and around the same time, the plants were introduced to North America by Chinese immigrants during the California gold rush. In China, paperwhites are known as water fairies and represent happiness. As fresh flowers are highly desirable during wintertime in the Northern Hemisphere, delicate-looking paperwhites are a perfect addition to Christmas and New Year's celebrations.

Like daffodils, paperwhites grow from bulbs, and they are perennials in much warmer climates than my prairie garden. The lovely thing about paperwhites is that you don't need to give the bulbs a chilling period before you pot them, which makes forcing them into bloom easy and quick, and a fun project to do during the holiday season!

You have a choice of planting paperwhites in water or in soil. If you decide to use water, find a shallow tray or bowl that is at least four inches deep. Fill half of the tray with a layer of glass beads (my favourite) or small stones. Tuck five to seven bulbs into the tray, packing them tightly together as this will make the best display when they bloom. Add water, but only enough to cover the roots. Don't immerse the bulbs themselves or you'll run into trouble with rotting. Place your tray near a window with bright—but not direct—sunlight and let the plants do their thing! It will take about two weeks for them to start sprouting in earnest, and another two or three weeks before you see blooms. Top the water off every few days.

If you prefer to grow paperwhites in soil, place them in a decorative container with sufficient drainage holes in the base. Fill the container about one quarter of the way with potting soil. Pack the bulbs tightly into the pot—this is not the time to worry about spacing—and cover them partway with soil. The soil should not cover the tops of the bulbs; leave the top quarter exposed. Water the bulbs. At this point they don't need any special care, just ensure the soil is damp but not soaking wet. Too much water will quickly rot the bulbs, so be cautious. When the shoots pop up, you can move the pots into a sunny spot. Paperwhites are very toxic, so if you have inquisitive cats and dogs, set the plants out of reach.

Probably the only annoying thing about paperwhites (other than the fragrance, if you find it too cloying) is that the leaves can grow very tall and untidily flop over. The trick for this? A shot of vodka. I'm not kidding. Researchers have discovered that regularly watering your paperwhites with a water and alcohol solution as the leaves are growing tricks the plant into thinking it is drought-stressed. The plant will respond by growing more compact foliage. If you're growing paperwhites in water instead of soil, just add the booze to the water itself. Bottoms up![52]—SN

POINSETTIA
Gift for the Newborn King and a Colourful Houseplant for North American Homes

Many years ago, I attended a greenhouse tour for one of the big commercial operations here in Alberta, Canada. One of their specialties was growing poinsettias for the local holiday market. I took in the sight of rows of thousands of near-perfect plants, all the same heights in their metallic green and red containers, the only difference being that some had red-coloured bracts (modified leaves that are often mistaken for flowers), some had cream-coloured bracts, and others were pink. That's not how poinsettias grow in the wild: in their native Mexico, they grow into rambling small trees that reach up to 15 feet (4.5 meters) in height.

Aztecs called poinsettias *cuetlaxochitle*, which means "purity." The plant was often found in medicines and used to produce dyes, but it was considered so important that commoners did not have permission to access it. Only religious leaders and rulers could. Each red bract was considered the blood of a person who had been sacrificed to the gods, and if the plants were healthy, that meant the gods were pleased. When Aztec civilization was devastated by Spanish explorers between 1519 and 1521, the importance of poinsettias, along with nearly everything else about Aztec culture, was pretty much lost.

The Catholic missionaries who had been installed in Mexico after the fall of the Aztecs brought new religious beliefs, including the story of the birth of the Christ Child, and that's when the poinsettia became culturally significant once again. Legend has it that a very poor Mexican girl visited a church on Christmas Eve and was distressed that she didn't have a worthy gift to bestow upon baby Jesus. She was told that any gift would do if she gave it out of love. She went out to the night and found a weed growing in the ditches. She picked the plant and brought

it to the church altar. Right before everyone's eyes, in what appeared to be a miracle, the green plants turned bright red. Thereafter, the poinsettia was known in Mexico as *flor de nochebuena*—flower of the blessed night. Other Central and South American countries began to celebrate the mystery of the poinsettia. But the plant wasn't yet a Christmas symbol in the United States until a man named Joel Poinsett made a serendipitous decision that would not only change the course of his life, but bring the plants that were eventually named after him into our homes during the holiday season.

Poinsett was a doctor, an amateur architect, a botanist, and a politician. Varied interests and a strong work ethic took him many places, including to Mexico as an American ambassador in the late 1820s, where he almost lost his job due to his unpopularity. During mass at a Mexican church on Christmas in 1824, he saw poinsettias for the first time. The plant's beauty and significance to the people captivated him. When he lost his appointment a year later, he had poinsettia cuttings with him on his return to the United States. Over time, his introduction of the plant to American Christmas traditions led to its widespread adoption.

First rule of poinsettia-keeping: if you purchase a plant when it is breathtakingly cold outside, ensure it is wrapped to the nines for transport so it doesn't get chilled. These plants can't handle cold drafts at all, so when you find that perfect place for it in your home, ensure the exterior door isn't anywhere nearby. Second rule: don't overwater your poinsettia. Remove that shiny foil sleeve the plants are typically sold with and set up a proper saucer so you can bottom water the plant. You'll need to strike a careful balance: allow the plant to dry out between waterings, but not so much that you cause drought-stress. Otherwise, keep your poinsettia in bright, indirect light and enjoy its colourful bracts (the actual flowers are those tiny little yellow structures in the middle of the bracts).[53]—SN

ROSEMARY
Queen of Herbs

You know it as a common medicinal and culinary herb, but it's easy to see why rosemary (*Salvia rosmarinus*) also has several ties to the holiday season. It has woody stems, needle-like silver-green leaves, a Christmas-tree-like growth habit (albeit in miniature) and delicious pine flavour when added to the Christmas bird, roasted root vegetables, or stuffing. Pots of rosemary add fragrance and beauty to the kitchen window, and if you live in a warm climate, you can decorate your patio, courtyard, or front steps with the plants. As you can likely guess by its common name, rosemary has a connection to Mary, mother of Jesus. When Mary spread her blue cloak over the white flowers of the plant, the blooms turned a brilliant blue colour and the plant was given the name "rose of Mary." If you want to maintain the best flavour of the plant's leaves for cooking, you'll need to trim the burgeoning blooms away, no matter how lovely they look. Keeping them will cause the plant to shift energy away from the leaves, which will mar the taste.

In warm climates, rosemary can grow into a short-lived shrub, about 5 feet (1.5 metres) tall. For those of us who can't successfully overwinter rosemary outdoors, we can make this herb part of our indoor edible garden as long as we can offer it bright, but indirect sunlight. High humidity in our winter homes is necessary to keep rosemary happy. Have a spray bottle filled with water ready to perform a misting whenever needed.[54]—SN

WHITE AND RED CARNATIONS
The Love and the Passion

Christmas colours are often white, red, and green. They have stood for snow, the red berries of holly and other fruit, and green for evergreen trees. Yet there is another reason why we think of white and red as Christmas colours, and it has to do with how Santa Claus in North America came to be dressed in what we might think of his traditional colours. In Europe, St. Nicolas or Father Christmas would be dressed in many different colours. But back in the early twentieth century Coca-Cola put out an ad with Santa Claus drinking a bottle of Coke. Well, Coca-Cola colours are red and white so they dressed Santa Claus in those colours too. And now the world over, in what ever variation he is known by, Santa Claus more often than not is dressed in red and white.

What has this to do with carnations you ask? Because we often include them in Christmas floral arrangements and seasonal foliage centerpieces. Carnations have many meanings, but in terms of the festive season, they have a special relevance. White carnations symbolize motherly love due to the legend that when Mary mother of Christ wept over the death of her son, her tears landed on soil which sprouted these soft white flowers. White also stands for innocence, purity, and love. Red carnations are often associated with love and passion.

Together with green evergreens, red and white carnations are an elegant and dynamic combination. On a more prosaic note, they also are long lasting and readily available, making it easy to tuck them into one or more of your seasonal arrangements. —JM

HOUSEPLANT ARRANGEMENTS

Creating Arrangements

Creating a seasonal plant container from some of the marvelous flowering and foliage plants available at this time of year is both rewarding and fun. As with all living plant arrangements or containers, the goal is to provide enough space for each plant to have access to the light, moisture, nutrients, and space it requires to be healthy. Choose plants with similar growing requirements, especially when it comes to water if you plan to grow them in the same container. Some of the plants we've discussed, including rosemary and poinsettia, will quickly go south if they are overwatered. Aim to have plants that require the soil to be almost dry before watering together, and place those that require consistently moist soil in another arrangement.

You are not limited to just the flowering plants of the season. Including tropical foliage is an option as they can be effective foils for the seasonal plants, not to mention becoming permanent residents in your home after the season has ended.

Select a container that is large enough for the plants you wish to include. It should have drainage so that overwatering is avoided. If it doesn't have drainage holes, then use a cache pot with drainage holes that is placed inside the larger container.

Choose plants that are an appropriate size for the container. You don't want a top-heavy container or one where the plants become lost. A good rule of thumb is that the container should be about one-third of the mass with the plants being two-thirds of the size of the planter.

Use good quality soilless growing media (a.k.a. potting soil) that has either perlite or pumice added for aeration and moisture retention, and fill the container about halfway. Remove plants from their pots, gently loosening their roots, and place them in the container. Arrange the plants as you wish to display them best. Consider whether the container is to be viewed from all sides or from one side. Plants should be visible from the best vantage point. Once you are happy with their placement, add more soil to snug the plants in place.

Water the arrangement from the bottom by placing the container in a saucer of water and letting the potting soil wick up the water. If all the water hasn't been absorbed in an hour, then drain away the excess. Consider adding a simple clay water sensor to the arrangement so that you can readily see when the soil is becoming dry and it is time to water again.

Containers of holiday plants can be augmented by carefully placed branches, twigs, and evergreen foliage, as well as pinecones. Additional decorations can also be included to contribute to the festive air of the arrangement.

Aftercare for Houseplant Arrangements

Plants can remain in the container so long as they continue to be happy and healthy. Continue with the careful watering regime, but fertilizer will not be required.

Once they start to grow or flowers have finished blooming, it may be time to disassemble the container and pot individual plants in their own containers. Carefully remove the plants from the container, disentangling any roots that may have intermingled. Place fresh potting soil in their new containers and allow them to settle in before starting a regime of fertilization once spring arrives. Some holiday plants can be allowed to go dormant—predominately amaryllis, cyclamen, and azalea—before they resume growth later in the year. Likewise, poinsettias can be pruned back once their colourful bracts have gone and grown as individual plants; they can even be planted outside in the summer months. Come fall, they can be subjected to a period of darkness to trigger their leaves to change colour in time for the new holiday season. —JM

Chapter 4.

The SWEET and SAVOURY SMELLS of the SEASON

Allspice

One of the warm, rich spices that make Christmas cakes so special is allspice (*Pimenta dioica*). It is a common flavour used in baking in North America and Europe, but it is widely used in savoury dishes such as rice and meat in Middle Eastern, Caribbean, and Latin American cuisines. Allspice is the dried berry of a tree in the myrtle family and is endemic to Jamaica. Christopher Columbus referenced the spice in his travels during the fifteenth century, and the commodity was quickly introduced to Europe thereafter. Ground allspice is typically used in baking, while the whole berry is sometimes tucked into jars of pickles (I use them in my pickled beet recipe) or added to soups and stews. Be sure to warn your diners about your allspice addition to their meal: no one wants to bite down on a dried allspice berry, as they'll need a rapid visit to the dentist! I keep whole allspice berries on hand and grind them when I need them for the freshest, most intense flavour. If you have access to allspice tree leaves, they can also be used in cooking; fresh leaves are often added to smoked meats or infused into soups.

If you're not living in a tropical climate, you can grow allspice in a greenhouse or conservatory. Bear in mind that you will need two plants—a male and a female—to set fruit, as allspice trees are dioecious. The trees can reach more than ten feet (three metres) tall in an indoor setting, and up to sixty feet (eighteen metres) in the wild.[55]—SN

Apples

Gardeners in temperate climates throughout the world can grow apples for their own wassail bowls, but some varieties are hardier than others and better suited to cold regions. On the Canadian prairies, where I live, several excellent apple varieties tolerate winters that are minus 40° F (minus 40° C) or colder and survive short, dry summers to produce delicious fruit. In warmer areas, such as Washington state and the interior of British Columbia, apples are commercially grown in abundance and are harvested and stored for months of good eating.

When growing apples, know that you need to have a pollinizer to ensure fruit set—that is, you need to plant a second apple or crabapple of a compatible variety nearby. Orchardists have their favourite pollinizers; those of us with one apple tree in an urban yard rely on our neighbours to have a suitable variety available in their gardens. Bees and other pollinators get the work of pollination done.

Apple trees can live a long time (the oldest worldwide have been documented at 200 to 300 years old, but you can generally expect up to 80). They will produce fruit for most of their lifetimes, making them wonderful investments in a garden space. Small-space gardeners can experiment with espaliering their trees and guaranteeing a successful harvest in a confined spot.—SN

Cinnamon

Cinnamon is one of the spices that is often found in wassail bowls. It is the bark of *Cinnamomum zeylanicum*, a small evergreen tree. Another cinnamon-flavoured spice is harvested from related plants called cassia. Cinnamon bark is dried and tightly rolled into sticks. The bark can be ground into a fragrant, sweet powder, and the oil is sometimes extracted for use in cooking. Cinnamon is native to Sri Lanka, then known as Ceylon, but the commodity was already on the move via Arabic trade in 2000 BCE, when it was first documented in Egypt. In the 1500s, Portuguese colonizers in Sri Lanka, followed by the Dutch and the British, worked the cinnamon trade for nearly four centuries, until Sri Lanka finally gained its independence in 1948. By this time, cassia had surpassed true cinnamon as the spice of choice (mostly because it is cheaper than true cinnamon). Today, most of the cinnamon you will find on the grocery store shelves is cassia, from countries such as Indonesia, the world's largest supplier.

Cassia isn't a plant North American gardeners can grow, as it is a resident of sub-tropical to tropical climates. It takes fifteen to twenty years for cassia trees to be ready for harvest, and during the harvesting process, they are cut down. The inner bark is the only part that is used by consumers, and it amounts to about seventy-seven pounds (thirty-five kilograms) of bark per tree. This entire process requires continual replanting of new cassia trees to annually replenish the harvest.[56]—SN

Cloves

Cloves (*Syzygium aromaticum*) are the unopened flower buds of Myrtaceae, an evergreen tree in the Myrtle family that is native to Indonesia. The buds are picked by hand then dried, which turns them a dark brown with a spicy, pungent aroma due to the presence of an aromatic oil, eugenol. The word *clove* is derived from the Latin *clavus* which means nail, and these small knobby spices look for all the world like tiny nails.[57]

As with many of the spices originating from the Spice Islands of Indonesia, cloves have been traded for thousands of years, with the source of this highly prized spice kept a secret to control both the supply and price. These days cloves are not so expensive as the trees are now also cultivated in East Africa and the Caribbean after seeds were smuggled out by a French missionary in the eighteenth century.

Cloves, being scarce for most of history, were used carefully and only for seasonal celebrations. The rich, warming flavour lends itself to cozy dishes such as gingerbread, fruitcake, plum pudding, mincemeat tarts, hot mulled cider, and wassail bowls. All those dishes were favourites of mine as a child and continue to be to this day.

Cloves are also used to create orange pomanders, which historically were carried to ward off smells and protect against illness, evil spirits, and just plain bad luck. The cloves help preserve the oranges, as they have anti-microbial properties, while the aromas of both ingredients mingle to create a lovely spicy citrus perfume that can be used to decorate the home. As a child, I would push the pointy end of cloves into the rind of oranges to make patterns and hang them in the tree. Today, I place them with a winter potpourri where they last throughout the holiday season.

To make an orange pomander, start by selecting your orange. Use a toothpick, skewer, or darning needle to pierce the rind to create a pattern that can be simple to fantastical. Then push the cloves into the holes. You can make a hanger by inserting a wire through the orange, tying it off at the bottom, and making a loop at the top. If you want your pomander last longer, make them a couple of weeks ahead of when you want to have them out (or give them away as gifts) and place the completed pomanders in a paper bag with some cinnamon dusted over it. The cloves will draw out the juices of the orange, shrinking it a bit, and cinnamon is an anti-fungal agent, too. This is such a lovely tradition and a beautiful gift; it is time that pomanders came back into our homes![58] —JM

Ginger

Who doesn't love ginger? Originating in southeast Asia, ginger (*Zingiber officinale*) has been domesticated since 3000 BCE, and is now a cultigen, no longer existing in its wild form. Ginger has been prized for its delightful aroma and flavour, used for its medicinal and culinary qualities as well as its spiritual properties.

Transported in pots from Southeast Asia to the Pacific Islands by the Austronesians, it then made its way to India. By the first century ACE, ginger was being traded to the Roman Empire and made its way across the continent, valued for both its herbal and culinary properties. In Medieval times, ginger was valued because it was believed to keep you warm during the cold winter months.

Ginger, often called ginger root, is not a root at all, but rather a rhizome or tuberous stem. It is an herbaceous perennial in tropical climates, sending up three-foot (one-metre) tall pseudostems with long, narrow light green leaves. Underground, the rhizomes become fat and knobby, with many branches and a thin, corky brown skin. Inside, the rhizomes are light yellow, with fibrous flesh that is juicy when the plant is young. Young rhizomes have a light aroma and zing, but as they age the flavour and heat of the volatile oils become more pronounced.

You can grow your own ginger plant indoors if you are in colder climes. Simply find a piece of the rhizome with fingers that have lots of nodes on it. If those nodes are starting to turn a light green, it is primed to go. After cutting a piece that has at least two nodes, allow it to callus over or dry for a couple of days before planting it in potting soil 1 inch (2.54 centimetres) deep with the eyes up. Place in a warm spot and keep the soil moist but not wet. Once sprouted, ginger needs nutrient-dense, warm soil, and lots of bright light to flourish. Harvest after a year and enjoy the spicy, piquant flavour of young ginger. Ginger is a quintessential spice for all things comforting at the end of the year, be it in wassail bowls or gingerbread, including gingerbread men and houses![59] —JM

Nutmeg

Nutmeg (*Myristica fragrans*) is an evergreen tree native to the Moluccas or Spice Islands of Indonesia, though these days it is also widely grown in the Caribbean. The nutmeg we use is the kernel of the seed of this tree, desirable for its pungent nutty, earthy, or musky aroma and slightly sweet taste due to the presence of the aromatic oil, myristicin.

Nutmeg has been known to the western world since at least the sixth century, with Arab traders bringing it overland to the Byzantium Empire, from where it made its way to the Roman Empire and beyond. Prized for its medicinal qualities and thought to prevent plague, nutmeg was also burned as incense. It quickly found its way into baking goods and to flavour many other dishes through the ages and around the world. Best freshly grated, nutmeg is one essential for spiced eggnog and wassail bowls alike. It's also marvelous in other meat and vegetables dishes, baked goods, and of course, pumpkin spice lattes!

Worth its weight in gold, as were many spices from exotic lands, its source was abruptly cut off when the Ottoman Turks conquered Constantinople and established their empire.[60] The race was on to find another route to source this and other spices. Many countries joined in the great exploration of sea routes to the Indies, which led to Christopher Columbus landing in the Americas in 1492, among other world-altering events. The Dutch East India Company arrived at the Spice Islands first and established colonial rule, seeking to keep the trade of nutmeg to themselves and prices high. However, a French horticulturist smuggled out some viable seeds, which were planted in Mauritius in the Caribbean. The rest is history as they say.

While nutmeg is the stone or seed of the tree, mace is derived from the crimson filaments surrounding the seed, called arils. It has its own distinctive flavour and colour. It is more intense than nutmeg but less sweet.

Nutmeg and mace are harvested once the fruit has split and drops to the ground. The arils, which become mace, are removed and dried, and the seeds in their shells are allowed to dry until they rattle in the shell, then are cracked open to remove the kernel.

Stored whole nutmeg can retain its flavour for quite some time. Simply grate the *nut* whenever you wish to add it to any dish, drink, or sweet. It is interesting to note that other species are also called nutmeg, but only the seed of *Myristica fragrans* is the spice we all enjoy.[61] —JM

Oranges

Oranges and other citrus fruit were already finding their way to England via trade channels at the tail end of the thirteenth century, so it would not have been completely unheard of to find dried citrus peel in a wassail bowl at that time. Six centuries later, Victorian England exploded in a frenzy of exploration which coincided with the cultivation of plants from all over the world, including the citrus fruit they grew in so-called orangeries, precursors to greenhouses that could protect plants that were not cold-hardy.

In North American households and in many places in Europe, Japanese and Chinese mandarin oranges (sometimes wrapped in green tissue paper as in days gone by) and clementines are a staple of holiday sideboards and are often found in the toes of stockings on Christmas morning. There is a wonderful story about how those oranges became a tradition. Saint Nicholas—the real person, who was from a well-to-do family and eventually became a bishop, later canonized by the Catholic church after his death in 343 ACE—became aware that his neighbour, a widower with three young daughters, was suffering from financial hardship. He snuck to their home in the middle of the night and threw three bags of gold coins into the window. Either his aim was really poor, or really good, as the coins landed in the girls' stockings where they were hung to dry after laundering. Sound like a familiar tale? Over retellings, oranges came to represent the gold coins.

Mandarin oranges and seedless clementines (bred from mandarins) are grown in North America in the warm climates of states such as Florida, Texas, Arizona, and California, and therefore Americans have the fortune of enjoying nationally grown fruit. China is currently the top supplier of mandarin oranges in the world, and nearly all of the so-called Christmas oranges Canadians find in their supermarkets are from China. While Canada's climate is too cold to grow oranges outdoors, even prairie-dwellers can grow small citrus fruit indoors in the dead of winter. Full sun during the summer months and plenty of humidity are needed to make these tiny trees happy. Their growing medium needs to have a slightly acidic pH, and extreme care must be taken not to overwater them.[62]—SN

Sage

A traditional herb that stuffing simply cannot be without is culinary sage (*Salvia officinalis*). The genus name comes from the Latin word *salvere*, meaning "to be saved," reflecting the herb's historical use as a meat preservative. The warm, slightly minty flavour (it is related to *Mentha* spp., after all) is particularly enjoyable when mixed with butter and citrus, and of course, in yeast bread. When it comes to stuffing the Christmas turkey or goose, a good old-fashioned sage and onion bread mixture is the best for a reason in my book: it tastes even better than the bird!

If you want to grow your own sage to use in holiday stuffing (or maybe as part of a sauce for ravioli, or meats such as venison, or veal the rest of the year), plant this hardy perennial in a sunny spot, and give it a fair amount of space, as it can reach a height and spread up to two feet (sixty centimetres) in ideal conditions. Sage will need some supplemental water when rainfall isn't enough, but it struggles in boggy soils, so ensure you offer it a well-drained location. Side-dress sage plants with a handful of compost in the spring and follow that up with another in the early summer. Harvest sage leaves on a regular basis (they make an amazing tisane!), and once the plant has matured, prune it to shape every spring, lopping off some of the woody branches that no longer produce well. While sage has beautiful spikes of purple blooms, if you are consuming the silver-coloured leaves, you'll want to trim the flowers away to maintain the flavour of the foliage.[63]—SN

Thyme

Thyme (*Thymus vulgaris*) is a member of the mint family, Lamiaceae. It is a sub-shrub with woody, wiry stems with small, dark green leaves that have a pungent aroma. If allowed to flower, in mid-summer it will bear pink, lavender, or white flowers that are real bee magnets. It loves sunny and dry locations, with somewhat lean soil. It grows equally well in in-ground beds or containers, and I always bring in a plant to grace my sunny windowsill for winter cooking.[64] —JM

TRADITIONAL STAPLES AND TREATS OF THE SEASON

THE WASSAIL BOWL
To Your Health!

The English tradition of wassailing, which dates to medieval times, took several forms of celebration over the centuries, with various additions and regional expressions. Essentially, if you hailed someone by shouting "Wassail," you were wishing them good health, but the whole idea developed into much more than that. In some parts of England, there were fire-wassails, which involved lighting thirteen fires in the winter fields after Christmas Eve to celebrate the twelve apostles and the Virgin Mary, or to represent the sun and the months of the year. In other parts of the country, hawthorn branches were bent into globe shapes in early January and burned in a fire-wassail on New Year's morning to bring in a fresh start to the new year.

The apple-wassail comes from traditions that ensured a good harvest from the orchard; the ceremony usually involved pouring hard apple cider into the roots and onto the trunks of the trees before harvest season. Sometimes songs were sung, and in some areas, the trees were beaten with sticks to ward off agents that could jeopardize the harvest.

The wassail bowl married the wishes of good health to the apple trees to the continued well-being of everyone during the holiday season and beyond. The original medieval wassail bowl did not contain any cider, but was a custardy concoction of baked apples, wine, sugar, spices, and eggs. Through the centuries, apple cider became a key ingredient, and nowadays, wassail bowls may contain several different types of non-alcoholic and alcoholic fruit-based punches. The custom of wassailing, to visit with strangers and friends alike, to share in the wassail bowl and be

rewarded with wassail cakes, originated as an exchange between feudal lords and their serfs—basically, the only time of the year when the poor were allowed to beg from their wealthy masters and obtain some reciprocal goodwill. Wassailing was usually done on Twelfth Night, in early January, but later became part of the Christmas carolling tradition.[65]—SN

MULLED WINE
A Drink of the Ages

Mulled wine is a centuries-old tradition, dating back to the beginnings of the Roman Empire and served as a drink to warm oneself in the cold months; it was also a special part of the Saturnalia festival. The drink is even older, though. In Ancient Greece it was called Hippocras after Hippocrates, the father of medicine.

It was made by simmering wine with honey, along with pepper, saffron, and laurel. Dates were often added too. Then the mixture was preserved by plunging hot coals into it. To serve, the mixture was blended in with red wine and enjoyed.

Fast forward to the fourteenth century, and the Roman *Conditum Paradoxum* was now simply the spiced wine of France and Spain, though made in the same way.[66] Often the wine was heated using a hot poker after the spices were added. Its use spread through Europe, where it evolved into many regional recipes, including *gluhwein* in Germany. In Scandinavian countries, mulled wine is *glogg*, spelled with variations in each country. In France, it is *vin chaud*. And all over the world warmed wine with spices has its own special name

In many a time, mulled wine was used to ward off a winter illness, using the medical properties of the spices. To this day a hot drink after a cold day is particularly welcome to ward off the chill. It wasn't until the late nineteenth century, though, that mulled wine became so closely associated with the Christmas season.

While there are many recipes for mulled wine, the essentials are the same. Simmer a young red wine with honey or brown sugar. Some recipes call for orange or lemon zest, and others for slices of orange in the mixture. Add whole spices, not ground. Cinnamon sticks, star anise, allspice, cloves, and pepper are common favourites. Allow to simmer for a while, then filter the drink to remove the spices and fruit. Serve warm, not hot. It is the spices that warm you up, not the actual temperature of the drink. —JM

JANET'S *favourite* RECIPE for a SIMPLE MULLED WINE

- 1 bottle of red wine, typically Merlot
- 2 small oranges, sliced
- 4 tablespoons (60 millilitres) of honey
- 2 cinnamon sticks
- 2 whole star anise
- 6 cloves

Simmer for 20 minutes, then strain and serve.

CHRISTMAS CAKE
A Very Special Fruitcake

Many cultures have a version of Christmas cake, but the one we're primarily going to talk about here dates to the sixteenth century and is English in origin. It wasn't a cake at first, but rather a porridge infused with plums, eaten on Christmas Eve after a day of fasting. It was a simple recipe, consisting of oatmeal and water, but as time went on, it was jazzed up to include even more dried fruit, spices, and honey. Finally, someone decided it didn't need to have oatmeal in it anymore and added proper cake ingredients: eggs, butter, and wheat flour. Nowadays, there are countless recipes for Christmas cake, some with marzipan, frosting or glazing, and mincemeat, as well as several variations containing whiskey, rum, or other alcohol. All of them feature seasonal dried fruit, such as apples, and they are heavy on the fragrant and sweet spices such as cinnamon and nutmeg. The spices and fruit flaunt the abundance of the harvest and celebrate the "exotic" spices that the Wise Men brought in the story of the nativity.

Many Christmas cakes are made up to three months in advance of the holiday season, as they firm up and become less crumbly during the wait (plus, this gives the baker time to frequently rub a bit of brandy, sherry, or other flavoured alcohol into the sides and top of the cake). The love and care bestowed upon this dessert are immense!

Although it is more of a tradition related to the baking of the Christmas pudding, rather than the cake, some bakers will also stir a coin into the Christmas cake batter. The lucky recipient is supposed to be granted luck in the coming year. Pennies were traditionally used when the custom began in the seventeenth century, and eventually sixpence became the popular denomination.[67]—SN

CRANBERRY SAUCE
The Perfect Companion

What would our traditional Christmas fare be without cranberry sauce? They go together like ham and eggs! But have they always been a tradition at festive dinners? Cranberries are a group of low, creeping, evergreen shrubs in the subgenus *Oxycoccus* in the *Vaccinium* in the heath or heather family, Ericaceae. They love acidic soil and boggy conditions that can be found across the cooler regions of the temperate Northern Hemisphere. While Europe has some native species, notably *Vaccinium oxycoccos*, in North America the species is likely to be the large cranberry, *V. macrocarpon*. Interestingly, they are related to blueberries, which enjoy the same growing conditions.

In North America, the history of cranberries stretches into the distant past. People have traditionally gathered the red, tart, and astringent cranberries for fresh and dried eating, as a preservation technique for meat, for medicinal applications, and as a dye for clothing. Cranberries are a symbol of peace and friendship often exchanged as an offering or consumed communally. While these berries are known by many names, the word *cranberries* came about because European settlers thought the pink flowers resembled cranes.[68] Over time, the crane berry was shortened to *cranberry*, though it has also been called bounceberry as fresh, ripe berries do bounce, as I well know when I drop them.[69]

Cranberries have been a sauce to accompany the traditional bird at both Thanksgiving and Christmas in Western cultures for some centuries, and I wouldn't have it any other way. Making cranberry sauce is quick, and it keeps well in the fridge from the Thanksgiving supper to that of the Christmas celebration. Leftover cranberry sauce also lends itself beautifully to baking, coffee cake being a particular favourite of mine.

JANET'S *Cranberry* SAUCE RECIPE

- 4 cups (950 grams) fresh cranberries
- Water, about 1 cup (250ml)—enough to just barely cover
- 1 cup (250ml) sugar

Put the cranberries, water, and sugar in a saucepan. Bring the liquid to a low simmer, and cook until the cranberries pop and can be mushed. Keep simmering until liquid is reduced. This takes about 15 minutes. Take off the stove and allow to cool and thicken. Have fun experimenting. I do!

Variations:

- I often use less sugar, as I like the sauce tart. You can also substitute honey, and I sometimes add in a bit of maple syrup for fun.
- Add in peeled and diced mandarin oranges, or exchange some of the liquid for orange juice.
- Add a dollop of orange liquor for an extra zing.

Cranberries have also been used since the nineteenth century to create garlands, by stringing popcorn and cranberries on threads and decorating the tree and house with the results. The strands are easy to make as long as you have patience, bakers twine, an embroidery needle with a blunt end, and good vision to thread the twine and fresh cranberries. Thread the needle with about three feet (one metre) of twine, and push the needle through each berry until you have enough on the strand. Knot both ends, and then make another one until you have enough strings to knot together into a long garland for the tree. To ensure that the garland will last through the season, spray it with a sealant and allow it to dry before hanging. Variations can include interspersing dried orange slices or popcorn. You can also make the berries appear frosted by dipping the garland in white glue and sprinkling either white sugar or Epsom salts on the berries.

You can also decorate the table with a centerpiece candle. Find a clear bowl or vase and fill with water. Add berries to the water along with some other bits of greenery if you like. The berries will float to the top and the greenery will sink below them. Then add a floating candle. Voila! You have an elegant centerpiece that takes no time at all to make.

You can even make a stovetop potpourri with cranberries, oranges, cinnamon sticks, whole cloves, and nutmeg to create a rich and spicy aroma that makes the whole house seem festive. Lovely red cranberries have boundless uses to decorate our homes and enliven our dinners. Thank heavens for these wonderful berries that mature just in time for the festivities![70] —JM

STUFFING FOR THE BIRD

Who doesn't love a stuffed turkey for a celebration? The tradition of stuffing dates back millennia, as evidenced by a 3,700-year old clay tablet found in present day Iraq, which inscribed recipes including one for flavoured bread to accompany poultry.[71] But it was the Ancient Romans that really got the culinary practice going with their love of stuffing all sorts of animals with a mixture of grains, such as spelt, vegetables, herbs, and spices.[72]

And the rest is history, as they say! There abounds many different styles of stuffing and thousands of recipes to accompany what is often poultry but can be other meats as well. It is an inexpensive side dish to augment the meal, especially the expensive meat. The dish is sometimes referred to as dressing, especially if it's cooked separately.

By the way, turkey is native to the Americas and was adopted as the traditional bird for Thanksgiving and Christmas by European settlers. They promptly exported live birds back to Europe, where they have been bred ever since. It was Henry VIII who first swapped out his goose for turkey as an expensive option.[73] It wasn't until the early twentieth century, however, that turkey became economical in the UK and the Christmas staple it is today. —JM

JANET'S *Traditional* ENGLISH STUFFING

My recipe for traditional English stuffing comes to me through my mother and her mother before her. It is simple and foolproof. Tucked inside the bird, the stuffing will absorb the flavour and juices of the turkey and create a lovely side dish.

Recipe for a 15 lb (7 kg) turkey.

- 1 loaf stale bread, preferably multigrain
- ½ cup butter
- 1 medium onion, chopped
- 2 sticks celery
- Sage to taste
- Thyme to taste
- Rosemary to taste
- Fresh pepper to taste
- 2 cups chicken stock
- Diced apple or bacon (optional)

Slice the bread and lightly toast it in the oven. Cut the slices up into cubes.

Sauté onions and celery in butter, and then add the sage, thyme, rosemary, and fresh pepper.

Add the cubes of bread and stir until they are nicely coated.

Moisten the whole mixture with chicken stock, preferably homemade broth.

Add diced apple or bacon if desired.

CANDY CANES
From Quiet Choirboys to a Million Dollar Industry

According to 2023 statistics, the familiar shepherd's crook-shaped white and red-striped peppermint sticks known as candy canes were the best-selling holiday candy in the United States, commandeering about 90 percent of the market. Whether they are used to decorate Christmas trees or shared at workplaces, parties, parades, or pretty much anywhere—even at my dentist's, which is an ingenious way to guarantee repeat business—cellophane-wrapped candy canes of all sizes are a sweet treat to look forward to in the holiday season. (And, if you want to do something a little different besides licking the J-shaped sticks, you can crush the candy up into cakes and cookies or use it to flavour hot chocolate or even martinis.)

The origin of candy canes is somewhat blurred by time and perspective, but regardless of the backstory, there are likely connections to Germany. One theory is that a frustrated choir-master in seventeenth-century Cologne used the candy to keep his restless young charges in line while they were working through the very long nativity mass. Another—and this time, documented—case recounts candy canes being used as decorations on a Christmas tree erected by a German-Swedish immigrant in Ohio in 1847. Around the same time, American cookbooks began to list recipes for making candy canes. Peppermint candies themselves were not new, of course—as a digestive aid, peppermint-infused medicines had long been available at apothecaries. But it was their unique J-shape that made candy canes so special.

What about that irresistible flavour of peppermint? That's from *Mentha × piperita*, a common garden perennial in many parts of the world. You may already have it growing in a partly sunny location in your own garden! Peppermint is delightfully easy to care for, as long as you give it supplemental water when there isn't sufficient precipitation. You can fertilize it once or twice per

growing season, but it will provide abundant flavourful foliage even in lean soil. Harvest the fresh leaves whenever you wish to; this encourages a dense growth habit and more yield. The leaves may be used fresh or dried for later use as peppermint tisane—a hot cup of which will be welcome in the bleak dreary days of winter. Mint species tend to spread aggressively, even in colder climates, so it is advisable to keep it in containers where it can't run roughshod all over the place.

If you're curious as to why peppermint seems cool on your tongue, it's all in the chemistry. Peppermint contains an alcohol called menthol, which triggers a reaction in the sensory neurons in your mouth when you eat it. While menthol itself is not cold, it tricks the brain into thinking it is, and we can't get enough!

And, for the adventurous, if you look hard enough online, you can find small manufacturers of candy canes for the discerning palate (or something like that). If you've ever wanted to try candy canes flavoured like hot dogs, gravy, macaroni and cheese, Caesar salad, or bacon, they're out there. I'll stick to peppermint, thank you very much.[74]—SN

CHESTNUTS
Decadent Delight

"Chestnuts roasting on an open fire" is the opening line of "The Christmas Song" first performed by Nat King Cole in 1946. It is an iconic favourite and brings to mind Christmases of a bygone age. Chestnuts have been valued in many cultures and cuisines over the centuries as have the magnificent chestnut trees that are found across the Northern Hemisphere from Asia to Europe to North America. The fruit of the chestnut, part nut, part vegetable, tastes like carrot when raw. But when roasted, it becomes a soft nutty flavorsome treat that begs to be peeled and popped in the mouth or made into various confections, sauces, and stuffings. Chestnuts are an essential ingredient for the traditional Christmas pudding from the UK, as well as *marron glace*, a French treat to be savoured.

Indeed, the chestnut acorn has been a staple food throughout the ages, with the trees called bread trees in many cultures for the abundant fruit that is ready to harvest from September through November.[75] The tradition of roasting the fruit of European or sweet chestnut (*Castanea sativa*) on braziers at markets throughout Europe long predates the song, and the tradition continued in the Americas where the abundant American chestnut (*Castanea dentata*) grew, with its small, flavourful acorns.

Unfortunately, in 1904 an Asian chestnut (*Castanea mollissima*) that was imported to Long Island, New York was found to be infected with a fungal disease called chestnut blight (*Cryphonectria parasitica*). Within forty years, virtually all the American chestnut trees, some 3.5 billion of them, perished throughout Canada and the United States.

All is not lost though as the search has been on since 1983 to develop a hybrid chestnut from both the Asian and American chestnut species that will have the Asian chestnut's resistance to the disease, alongside the attributes of the American chestnut.[76]

So far, the resistance developed is not sufficient to attempt large scale replanting of the hybrids, but work is continuing toward the goal of re-establishing the chestnut forests of America. In the meantime, we can enjoy chestnuts imported from Asia and continue the tradition celebrated in song. —JM

To roast chestnuts, start by buying the freshest fruit you can find. They should be shiny, clean and heavy for their size. Wipe each fruit with a damp cloth to remove any debris, then score an X on the rounded side of the shell. This will allow steam to escape while being roasted. If you neglect to do so or don't go all the way through the shell, you may have exploding chestnuts. A nice mess to clean up!

Pop them in a preheated oven at 425° F (215° C) on cookie sheets, with the X side facing up. Roast them until the shells peel back from the X and the meat inside shows a nice caramel colour. Usually, the roasting time is around thirty minutes, but it will depend on the size of the acorns, so start checking after ten minutes, peeking in to see how things are progressing.

Once done, allow to cool somewhat before eating as they will be very hot! Burned tongues and fingers are not part of the tradition. Enjoy them straight out of the oven or in one of your favourite dishes of the season.[77]

POMEGRANATE
Jewel of Winter

I'm of the age where I don't particularly like to talk about how old I am, so I'll let you extrapolate the days I've been on the planet when I say I didn't actually taste a pomegranate until I was a young teenager. As a child growing up in northern Alberta, pomegranates were a very rare fruit, something you truly only saw at Christmastime. They were so prohibitively expensive that the average household could not fill a bowl with them and leave them on the table for everyone to enjoy throughout the season. Nowadays, you can get them in the big box stores year-round and if you don't want to peel them and go through the hassle of extracting the juicy blood-red arils yourself, you can purchase the seeds handily crammed into small clear plastic containers. Pomegranates are still very expensive, however, and I still tend to purchase them only during the holiday season. There's something about the extra infusion of vitamin C that the fruit practically oozes that feels especially welcome during the wintertime.

Pomegranate (*Punica granatum*) has a genus named for Carthage, a city in Tunisia famous for its trade in the fruit, and a species epithet fittingly meaning *seeded*. You've probably already figured out that the common name has to do with apples and seeds, and as pomegranates enjoyed the nickname Apple of Carthage for a time, that makes sense. Pomegranates are native to northern India and Persia (modern day Iran) and have likely been cultivated since 3000 BCE. Phoenician exploration brought the fruit to Tunisia and Egypt, and through expanding trade channels, pomegranates eventually made their way to China, into the Roman Empire, and to the Mediterranean. By the late eighteenth century, they were being cultivated in the Americas, and you'll now find them commercially grown in states such as California and Florida.

According to Greek myth, Persephone, the daughter of Demeter, goddess of the harvest, was kidnapped one day by Hades, god of the underworld. Demeter searched for her daughter for days but could not find her. In her devastation, Demeter caused every growing plant to wither and die. In the meantime, Hades and Persephone were getting along just fine in the underworld. Demeter finally figured out where her daughter was and demanded that she return to the land of the living. When a juicy fresh pomegranate was offered to Persephone, she knew she shouldn't eat it (if you eat or drink anything in the underworld, you are trapped there forever). Depending on which version of the story you read, Persephone was either tricked by Hades or chose of her own volition (I like the latter variation as it gives Persephone some agency) to eat six pomegranate seeds. The result: Demeter gets to see her daughter six months out of the year, when spring and summer are in the world, while Persephone joins Hades in his dark and dreary kingdom the rest of the year, during the winter, when Demeter is stricken with grief once more.

In ancient Persia, Zoroastrian believers valued pomegranates as a symbol of the soul's immortality and the "glow of life," the cycle of life, death, and rebirth. Even in modern times, eating a pomegranate on Shab-e Yalda, the eve of the winter solstice, hearkens back to the idea of the victory of the sun over the darkness of winter. A beautiful flavourful soup called *ash-e anar*, filled with glistening pomegranate arils, is often served.

In Greece, a long-standing tradition concerns pomegranates and the New Year's "first footings" concept. In households that attend church, a pomegranate fruit may be taken to the service to be blessed; regardless, once the clock strikes midnight on New Year's Eve, the whole family gathers outside in the dark. The head of the household or a designate uses their right hand to smash a pomegranate fruit against the door of the house, with the goal that the arils fly everywhere. The more seeds that scatter, the more fortune the family will have in the new year. Then the family proceeds to enter the house right foot first, and the remaining pieces of the pomegranate fruit are shared and eaten. And that's the part I love most about pomegranates: the fact that they can be shared among many celebrants, all the seeds pieces of community and connection.[78]—SN

Conclusion

And a PARTRIDGE in a PEAR TREE

The end of the year has been celebrated with religious rites and great festivals for centuries. In medieval times, the Christmas festivities spanned a full twelve days, starting with December 25, honouring the nativity and Christmastide, and ending with the Eve of Epiphany on January 5 (January 6 being Three Kings Day, when the Magi traditionally arrived in Bethlehem). Both secular and religious celebrations occur throughout the days stretching both sides of New Year's Day and climaxing with a feast on the Twelfth Night.

The twelve religious and feast days of the season have forever been captured by the song "The Twelve Days of Christmas," that was originally a folk song or children's counting game. In 1909, Frederic Austin wrote the version that is now the popular Christmas carol.

The pear tree is immortalized as the tree that the partridge sits in on the first day of the festivities. As the song goes, "On the first day of Christmas my true love gave to me / A partridge in a pear tree." From time immemorial mankind has celebrated the pear tree for its beauty and fruit. The pear tree is a long-lived tree and in many cultures has represented longevity, wisdom, fruitfulness, and divine sustenance.

Pears (*Pyrus* spp.) are native across Asia to North Africa and Western Europe. They are generally medium-sized trees maturing at roughly sixty-five feet (twenty metres). They have simple dark green leaves of an oval shape and glossy appearance.

The flowers are white with five petals and numerous stamens and are sweetly fragrant. The fruit is a pome—like the apple that the genus is related to—that matures in late summer and fall. Many pear varieties store very well and are a seasonal delight for the holidays. —JM

May we all celebrate the season with its rich heritage of traditions and customs, where the plants that contribute to the festivities add their symbolism, aromas, and bounty. May we rejoice in the renewal of the light and anticipate the rebirth of the land as the year moves past the winter solstice, the religious festivals, through to New Years Day and the Twelfth Night. —JM & SN

ACKNOWLEDGEMENTS

Janet and Sheryl: Creating this book was both a delightful gift and an exciting challenge, which we couldn't resist (honestly, we love any excuse to celebrate plants!). A huge thank you to our massively supportive, talented, and dedicated team at TouchWood Editions: Tori Elliott (publisher), Nara Monteiro (editorial coordinator), Curtis Samuel (publicist and social media coordinator), Kaiya Smith Blackburn (copy editor), Senica Maltese (proofreader), and Pat Touchie (owner). Thank you to Jazmin Welch, for the extraordinary art and design.

Sheryl: I am grateful to everyone who has created magic for me, not just during the holiday season, but throughout my life. We all need a little light, and I hope I can reciprocate by sharing a little of my own.

Janet: At this time of year, there is a pause in the busyness of life to reflect, to take time to renew and connect with the cycle of the seasons. It is also a time to give thanks for all who are part of my circle of life: family, friends, colleagues, and all those gardeners I connect with throughout the year. You are all so supportive of my work and are part of the magic of gardening, no matter the season.

NOTES

1. Boeckmann, "What is the Winter Solstice, and What is it All About?" Old Farmer's Almanac (website); O'Kelly and Claire, "Newgrange," Newgrange (website); "Dongzhi Festival: Chinese Winter Solstice Festival," China Highlights (website); "Celebrating Winter Solstice the Chinese Way," Eating Better (website); "The Pleiades: Cultural Stories of the Seven Sisters," Night Sky Tourist (website); McClure, "The Pleiades—or 7 Sisters—Known Around the World," EarthSky (website); "The Magical Feast of Juul, Celebrate the Shortest Day of the Year," Cosmic Deva (website); Wasserman, "World Population by Religion: A Global Tapestry of Faith," Population Education (website).
2. "Embracing Tradition: The Story Behind the Yule Log," Coeur de Xocolate (website).
3. Boeckmann, "What Is Yule? What Is a Yule Log?" Old Farmer's Almanac (website). Allen, *Decking the Halls*, 43–49.
4. "Oak Mythology and Folklore," Trees for Life (website).
5. Stritch, "Plants of the Winter Solstice," USDA Forest Service Department of Agriculture.
6. "Celtic Tree Calendar," Tree2mydoor (website); "Birch Tree Symbolism: Renewal and New Beginnings," Gaiansoul (website); Hopman, *The Sacred Herbs of Yule and Christmas*, 142–45.
7. McKeown, "The Holy Thorn: In Glastonbury, England, a Special Hawthorn Tree Blooms Every Year at Christmas," Catholic News Agency (website); "Glastonbury Thorn: Legendary English Hawthorn," Greenmantle Nursery (website).
8. "Saturnalia: Meaning, Festival & Christmas," HISTORY (website); Collins, *Stories Behind the Great Traditions of Christmas*, 113–17, McCoy, "Yaupon, A Native American Tea," James City County Williamsburg Master Gardener Association (website).
9. "English Ivy," Annafranklinblog, (website); "Ivy: Description, Plant, Species, and Facts," Encyclopaedia Britannica (website).
10. "Mistletoe," Wisconsin Horticulture (website); "Mistletoe: Plant, Poison, Major Species, and Christmas," Encyclopaedia Brittanica (website); "Mistletoe," The Canadian Encyclopedia (website); Wright, "Mistletoe Is a Parasitic, Explosive Plant That Maybe You Shouldn't Stand Underneath," Atlas Obscura (website).
11. Dostler, "The Christmas Rose," Plantscapers (website).
12. Borland, Plants of Christmas, 19; Allen, *Decking the Halls*, 71–73.
13. Hodgson, "The Christmas Plant That Came in From the Cold," Laidback Gardener (website); Greenbelt Indigenous Botanical Survey (website), "Wintergreen."
14. Collins, *Stories Behind the Great Traditions of Christmas*, 70–75; Ardagh, *The Truth About Christmas*, 5–7.

15. Heeringa, "The Real Reason Balsam Firs Are Desirable Christmas Trees," Green Bay Press-Gazette (website).
16. "Balsam Fir," National Christmas Tree Association (website); "Balsam Fir," Herbs 2000 (website).
17. "Concolor Fir (White Fir)," National Christmas Tree Association (website); "Why Should You Choose a Concolor Christmas Tree?" Agway of Cape Cod (website).
18. "The Firs: The Best Christmas Trees," National Forest Foundation (website).
19. "Douglas Fir," National Christmas Tree Association (website); Sweeton and Sweeton, *Christmas Trees & Holiday Greens*, 55–56.
20. "Fraser Fir," National Christmas Tree Association (website).
21. "Grand Fir," National Christmas Tree Association (website).
22. "Scots Pine: Ontario Invasive Plant Council," Ontario Invasive Plant Council (website).
23. Feather, "Tips for Selection and Care of Cut Christmas Trees," Penn State Extension (website).
24. Nafie, "24 Tips for Choosing the Perfect Christmas Tree," The Spruce (website); Sweeton and Sweeton, *Christmas Trees & Holiday Greens*, 60–65.
25. "Selecting a Christmas Tree," Christmas Tree Farmers of Ontario (website).
26. "Christmas Tree Care," Ontario Farm Grown Christmas Trees (website); Sweeton and Sweeton, *Christmas Trees & Holiday Greens*, 25–26.
27. Sweeton and Sweeton, *Christmas Trees & Holiday Greens*, 65–66.
28. U'mista Cultural Society Synthescape Art Imaging (website), "The Tree of Life: Cedar—Education—Living Tradition, the Kwakwaka'wakw Potlatch on the Northwest Coast."
29. "From Coast to Coast," Longhouse Specialty Forest Products (website).
30. "Western Red Cedar: Description & Facts," Encyclopaedia Britannica (website); "Incense Cedar," Encyclopaedia Britannica (website); Sweeton and Sweeton, *Christmas Trees & Holiday Greens*, 28–29.
31. "Eucalyptus: Description, Major Species, and Uses," Encyclopaedia Britannica (website); "Eucalyptus (Silver Dollar)," Floralife (website).
32. Rickman, "12 Grapes at Midnight: Spain's Unique New Year's Eve Tradition," Food Republic (website).
33. McAlpine, "How to Plant and Grow Magnolia Trees," Better Homes & Gardens (website).
34. "Which Kind of Christmas Tree Is for You," Milberger Nursery (website).
35. "Noble Fir," National Christmas Tree Association (website).
36. "Salal: *Gaultheria Shallon*," Biodiversity of the Central Coast (website)
37. "Amabilis Fir: Province of British Columbia," Ministry of Forests (website);"Abies Alba (Common Silver Fir, European Silver Fir, Silver Fir)," North Carolina Extension Gardener Plant Toolbox (website).
38. "Eastern White Pine," Ontario.ca.
39. Allen, *Decking the Halls*, 37–41.
40. "The History of the Christmas Wreath," Agriculture for Life (website).

41. Allen, *Decking the Halls*, 37–41.
42. Sweeton and Sweeton, *Christmas Trees & Holiday Greens*, 43–45.
43. "Garland: Floral Arrangement, Bouquet and Wreath," Encyclopaedia Britannica (website).
44. "Garland Galore: A History of Festive Foliage and Christmas," Rent-a-Christmas (website).
45. Sweeton and Sweeton, *Christmas Trees & Holiday Greens*, 37–39.
46. Sweeton and Sweeton, *Christmas Trees & Holiday Greens*, 12–13; "The Uniqueness of Amaryllis for the Christmas Season," Thursd (website); "Growing and Caring for Amaryllis," University of Minnesota Extension.
47. Rankel, "What Do Christmas Cactus Flowers Mean?" Greg App (website).
48. Iannotti, "How to Care for Christmas Cactus," The Spruce (website); Sweeton and Sweeton, *Christmas Trees & Holiday Greens*, 15–16; Rastch and Muller-Ebeling, *Pagan Christmas: The Plants, Spirits and Rituals at the Origins of Yuletide*, 84–85.
49. Goudy, "The Meaning of Cyclamen at Christmas," The Flower Writer (website).
50. VanZile and Aloi, "How to Grow and Care for Kalanchoe," The Spruce (website).
51. "How Do I Care for a Norfolk Island Pine?" Iowa State University and Extension.
52. "Paperwhites Are a Christmas and Chinese New Year Staple," Seed World Group (website); Grant, "Using Alcohol for Forced Bulbs: Keeping Amaryllis, Paperwhite, and Other Bulbs Upright," Gardening Know How (website).
53. Collins, *Stories Behind the Great Traditions of Christmas*, 152–57.
54. "Rosemary: Christmas Herb." Ricardo Cuisine (website).
55. Alfaro, "What Is Allspice?" The Spruce Eats (website).
56. "Cinnamon," Kew Gardens (website); Jones, "All About Cinnamon," 88 Acres (website).
57. "Exploring Cloves: The Christmas Spice," Delishably (website).
58. "Clove," Encyclopaedia Britannica (website); "Plants That Changed the World: Cloves," Fairchild Tropical Botanic Garden (website).
59. "Why Ginger Is at the Root of Holiday Traditions," Purdue University College of Agriculture (website); "Ginger, *Zingiber Officinale*," Wisconsin Horticulture.
60. Lum, "Nutmeg: Dark History of the Christmas Spice and My Favorite Recipes," Delishably (website).
61. "Nutmeg: Tree, Uses, History, Description, and Facts," Encyclopaedia Britannica (website).
62. "A Brief History of Clementines at Christmas," Toast (website); "Which Country Produces the Most Mandarines?" Helgi Library.
63. "Sage," McCormick Science Institute (website).
64. Ianotti, "How to Grow and Care for Thyme," The Spruce (website).
65. Raedisch, *The Old Magic of Christmas*, 227–28.
66. "Roman Wine: Conditum paradoxum," Eat History (website).
67. "Christmas Cake," British Food: A History (website).

68. “9 Things That You May or May Not Know About Cranberries,” Patience Fruit & Co. (website).
69. “Cranberries,” Department of Agriculture: New Jersey.
70. Allen, *Decking the Halls*, 80.
71. Tomczak, “The Ancient Roman Origins of Stuffing,” Tasting Table (website).
72. “Why Do We Eat Turkey at Christmas? Where It Came From.” Owton’s (website).
73. Rousseau and Hislop, “The History of Candy Canes and Why They Taste So Cool,” The Conversation (website).; Kennedy, “Who Invented Candy Canes?” HISTORY (website).
74. Stovell, “The Nutty Tradition: Chestnuts: A Global Christmas Delicacy,” cheffernandostovell.com (website); Morgan, “Why Don’t We Roast Chestnuts for the Holidays Anymore?” 10Best (website).
75. “American Chestnut,” Ontario.ca (website).
76. USDA Forest Service, “New Research Reveals Major Difference in Genomes of American and Chinese Chestnuts,” Phys.org (website).
77. Miller, “The Greek Myth You Should Know Before You Eat Any More Pomegranate Seeds,” Mashed (website); “Why Greeks Break a Pomegranate on New Year’s Day,” XpatAthens (website); Mirjalili (website), “Seeding Pomegranates: Yalda, Winter Solstice and Living With the Dead”; “5 Things You Didn’t Know About Pomegranates,” Kew Gardens (website).

BIBLIOGRAPHY

Agriculture for Life (website). "The History of the Christmas Wreath." December 10, 2023. agricultureforlife.ca/post/the-history-of-the-christmas-wreath.

Alfaro, Danilo. "What Is Allspice?" The Spruce Eats (website). June 11, 2024. thespruceeats .com/what-is-allspice-p2-995556.

Allen, Linda. *Decking the Halls*. Wisconsin: Willow Creek Press, 2000.

Agway of Cape Cod (website). "Why Should You Choose a Concolor Christmas Tree?" April 10, 2024. agwaycapecod.com/concolor-christmas-trees/.

Annafranklinblog (website). "English Ivy." Hearth Witchery. December 29, 2022. annafranklinhearthwitch.wordpress.com/2022/12/30/english-ivy/.

Ardagh, Philip. *The Truth About Christmas: Its Traditions Unraveled*. London: MacMillan Children's Books, 2012.

Biodiversity of the Central Coast (website). "Salal: Gaultheria Shallon." September 18, 2024. centralcoastbiodiversity.org/salal-bullnbspgaultheria-shallon.html.

Boeckmann, Catherine. "What is the Winter Solstice, and What is it All About?" Old Farmer's Almanac (website). August 23, 2024. almanac.com/content/first-day-winter -winter-solstice.

———."What Is Yule? What Is a Yule Log?" Old Farmer's Almanac (website). December 4, 2023, almanac.com/content/what-yule-log-christmas-traditions.

Borland, Hal. *Plants of Christmas*. Syracuse: Thomas Y. Crowell Junior Books, 1969.

British Food: A History (website). "Christmas Cake." November 14, 2021. britishfoodhistory .com/2011/12/05/christmas-cake/.

The Canadian Encyclopedia (website). "Mistletoe." September 18, 2024. thecanadian encyclopedia.ca/en/article/mistletoe.

China Highlights (website). "Dongzhi Festival: Chinese Winter Solstice Festival." September 18, 2024. chinahighlights.com/festivals/winter-solstice.htm.

Christmas Tree Farmers of Ontario (website). "Selecting a Christmas Tree." 2003. christmastrees.on.ca/index.php?action=display&cat=34&doc=How_to_Select_A _Christmas_Tree.pdf.

Coeur de Xocolate (website). "Embracing Tradition: The Story Behind the Yule Log." September 18, 2024. coeurdexocolat.com/yule-log-1.

Collins, Ace. *Stories Behind the Great Traditions of Christmas*. Michigan: Zondervan, 2003.

Cosmic Deva (website). "The Magical Feast of Juul, Celebrate the Shortest Day of the Year." December 19, 2017. shorturl.at/1mZtO.

Delishably (website). "Exploring Cloves: The Christmas Spice." September 18, 2024. delishably.com/spices-seasonings/All-About-Spices-The-Flavors-of-Christmas -Cloves.

Department of Agriculture: New Jersey (website). "Cranberries." 2021. nj.gov/agriculture /farmtoschool/documents/seasonality-chart/F2S%20Cranberries.pdf.

Dostler, Gina. “The Christmas Rose.” Plantscapers (website). June 27, 2023. plantscapers.com/the-christmas-rose/.

Eat History (website). “Roman Wine: Conditum paradoxum.” August 9, 2021. www.historicalcookingclasses.com/roman-wine-conditum-paradoxum/.

Eating Better (website). “Celebrating Winter Solstice the Chinese Way.” December 5, 2023. eating-better.org/news-and-reports/news/dongzhi-delights-celebrating-winter-solstice-the-chinese-way/.

Encyclopaedia Britannica (website). “Clove.” September 18, 2024. britannica.com/plant/clove.

———. “Eucalyptus: Description, Major Species, and Uses.” September 14, 2024. britannica.com/plant/Eucalyptus.

———. “Garland: Floral Arrangement, Bouquet & Wreath.” September 6, 2024. britannica.com/art/garland-floral-decoration.

———. “Incense Cedar: Evergreen, Coniferous, Fragrant.” July 20, 1998. britannica.com/plant/incense-cedar.

———. “Ivy: Description, Plant, Species, and Facts.” Encyclopedia Britannica. July 20, 1998. britannica.com/plant/ivy-plant.

———. “Mistletoe: Plant, Poison, Major Species, and Christmas.” August 14, 2024. britannica.com/plant/mistletoe.

———. “Nutmeg: Tree, Uses, History, Description, and Facts.” August 12, 2024. britannica.com/topic/nutmeg.

———. “Western Red Cedar: Description and Facts.” July 20, 1998. britannica.com/plant/Western-red-cedar.

Fairchild Tropical Botanic Garden (website). “Plants That Changed the World: Cloves.” July 17, 2024. fairchildgarden.org/visit/plants-that-changed-the-world-cloves-how-a-mysterious-spice-made-its-way-into-the-world/.

Feather, Sandy. “Tips for Selection and Care of Cut Christmas Trees.” Penn State Extension (website). extension.psu.edu/tips-for-selection-and-care-of-cut-christmas-trees.

Floralife (website). “Eucalyptus (Silver Dollar).” November 30, 2022. floralife.com/flowers/eucalyptus-silver-dollar/.

Gaiansoul (website). “Birch Tree Symbolism: Renewal and New Beginnings.” July 28, 2024. gaiansoul.com/plants-and-trees/birch-tree-symbolism-renewal-and-new-beginnings/.

Goudy, Ruth. “The Meaning of Cyclamen at Christmas.” The Flower Writer (website). December 21, 2021. ruthgoudy.com/the-meaning-of-cyclamen-at-christmas/.

Grant, Bonnie L. “Using Alcohol for Forced Bulbs: Keeping Amaryllis, Paperwhite, and Other Bulbs Upright.” Gardening Know How (website). April 28, 2022. gardeningknowhow.com/ornamental/bulbs/bgen/using-alcohol-forced-bulb.htm.

Greenbelt Indigenous Botanical Survey (website). “Wintergreen.” February 5, 2025. gibsurvey.ca/species/wintergreen.

Greenmantle Nursery (website). “Glastonbury Thorn: Legendary English Hawthorn.” September 18, 2024. greenmantlenursery.com/glastonburythorn.htm.

Heeringa, Coggin. "The Real Reason Balsam Firs Are Desirable Christmas Trees." Green Bay Press-Gazette. November 30, 2016. greenbaypressgazette.com/story/news/local/door-co/entertainment/2016/11/30/real-reason-balsam-firs-desirable-christmas-trees/94570880/.

Helgi Library (website). "Which Country Produces the Most Mandarins?" September 18, 2024. helgilibrary.com/charts/which-country-produces-the-most-mandarines/.

Herbs 2000 (website). "Balsam Fir." April 7, 2025. www.herbs2000.com/herbs/herbs_balsam_fir.htm.

HISTORY (website). "Saturnalia: Meaning, Festival & Christmas." September 14, 2022. history.com/topics/ancient-rome/saturnalia.

Hodgson, Larry. "The Christmas Plant That Came in From the Cold." Laidback Gardener (website). November 24, 2023. laidbackgardener.blog/2023/11/24/the-christmas-plant-that-came-in-from-the-cold/.

Hopman, Ellen Evert. *The Sacred Herbs of Yule and Christmas*. Vermont: Destiny Books, 2023.

Iannotti, Marie. "How to Care for Christmas Cactus." The Spruce (website). August 6, 2024. thespruce.com/christmas-cactus-4176983.

———. "How to Grow and Care for Thyme." The Spruce (website). August 5, 2024. thespruce.com/how-to-grow-thyme-1402630.

Iowa State University and Extension (website). "How Do I Care for a Norfolk Island Pine?" September 18, 2024. yardandgarden.extension.iastate.edu/faq/how-do-i-care-norfolk-island-pine.

Jones, Sam. "All About Cinnamon." 88 Acres (website). June 11, 2024. shorturl.at/g1YvZ.

Kew Gardens (website). "5 Things You Didn't Know About Pomegranates." September 18, 2024. kew.org/read-and-watch/surprising-pomegranate-facts.

———. "Cinnamon." September 18, 2024. kew.org/plants/cinnamon.

Kennedy, Lesley. "Who Invented Candy Canes?" HISTORY (website). August 30, 2023. history.com/news/candy-canes-invented-germany.

Longhouse Specialty Forest Products (website). "From Coast to Coast." March 26, 2021 longhousecedar.com/from-coast-to-coast/.

Lum, Linda. "Nutmeg: Dark History of the Christmas Spice and My Favorite Recipes." Delishably (website). November 24, 2022. delishably.com/spices-seasonings/All-About-the-Flavors-of-Christmas-Nutmeg.

McAlpine, Lynn. "How to Plant and Grow Magnolia Trees." Better Homes & Gardens (website). December 6, 2023. bhg.com/gardening/trees-shrubs-vines/trees/how-to-grow-magnolia-trees-281474979765643/.

McClure, Bruce. "The Pleiades—or 7 Sisters—Known Around the World." EarthSky (website). November 26, 2023. earthsky.org/favorite-star-patterns/pleiades-star-cluster-enjoys-worldwide-renown/.

McCormick Science Institute (website). "Sage." September 18, 2024. mccormickscienceinstitute.com/resources/culinary-spices/herbs-spices/sage.

McCoy, Elizabeth. "Yaupon, A Native American Tea." James City County Williamsburg Master Gardener Association (website). Updated April 1, 2024. jccwmg.org/wordpress/yaupon-a-native-american-tea/.

McKeown, Jonah. "The Holy Thorn: In Glastonbury, England, a Special Hawthorn Tree Blooms Every Year at Christmas." Catholic News Agency. August 17, 2024. catholicnewsagency.com/news/253143/the-glastonbury-thorn-a-resurrected-symbol-of-christmas.

Milberger Nursery (website). "Which Kind of Christmas Tree Is for You?" August 28, 2024. milbergernursery.com/educational/nordman-fir/.

Miller, Robin. "The Greek Myth You Should Know Before You Eat Any More Pomegranate Seeds." Mashed (website). April 1, 2021. mashed.com/372274/the-greek-myth-you-should-know-before-you-eat-any-more-pomegranate-seeds/.

Ministry of Forests. "Amabilis Fir: Province of British Columbia." January 25, 2024. 2.gov.bc.ca/gov/content/industry/forestry/managing-our-forest-resources/silviculture/tree-species-selection/tree-species-compendium-index/amabilis-fir.

Mirjalili, Faranak. "Seeding Pomegranates: Yalda, Winter Solstice and Living With the Dead." May 17, 2024. faranakmirjalili.net/articles/2022/12/25/seeding-pomegranates-yalda-winter-solstice-and-living-with-the-dead.

Morgan, Kate. "Why Don't We Roast Chestnuts for the Holidays Anymore?" 10Best (website). December 16, 2020. 10best.usatoday.com/interests/food-culture/how-roasted-chestnuts-became-extinct-christmas-tradition/.

Nafie, Coral. "24 Tips for Choosing the Perfect Christmas Tree." The Spruce (website). November 16, 2021. thespruce.com/choosing-the-perfect-christmas-tree-1976375.

National Christmas Tree Association (website). "Balsam Fir." August 1, 2019. realchristmastrees.org/education/tree-varieties/balsam-fir/.

———. "Concolor Fir (White Fir)." August 1, 2019. realchristmastrees.org/education/tree-varieties/concolor-fir-white-fir/.

———. "Douglas Fir." August 1, 2019. realchristmastrees.org/education/tree-varieties/douglas-fir/.

———. "Fraser Fir." August 1, 2019. realchristmastrees.org/education/tree-varieties/fraser-fir/.

———. "Grand Fir." August 1, 2019. realchristmastrees.org/education/tree-varieties/grand-fir/.

———. "Noble Fir." August 1, 2019. realchristmastrees.org/education/tree-varieties/noble-fir/.

National Forest Foundation (website). "The Firs: The Best Christmas Trees." April 19, 2022. nationalforests.org/blog/the-firs-the-best-christmas-trees.

Night Sky Tourist (website). "The Pleiades: Cultural Stories of the Seven Sisters." February 6, 2023. nightskytourist.com/pleiades/.

North Carolina Extension Gardener Plant Toolbox (website). "Abies Alba (Common Silver Fir, European Silver Fir, Silver Fir)." plants.ces.ncsu.edu/plants/abies-alba/.

O'Kelly, Claire. "Newgrange." Newgrange (website). September 18, 2024. newgrange.com/description.htm.

Ontario.ca (website). "American Chestnut." September 18, 2024. ontario.ca/page/american-chestnut-species-risk.

———. "Eastern White Pine." September 18, 2024. ontario.ca/page/eastern-white-pine.

Ontario Farm Grown Christmas Trees (website). "Christmas Tree Care." September 18, 2024. christmastrees.on.ca/index.php?action=display&cat=34.

Ontario Invasive Plant Council (website). "Scots Pine: Ontario Invasive Plant Council." February 14, 2024. ontarioinvasiveplants.ca/invasive-plants/species/scots-pine/.

Owton's (website). "Why Do We Eat Turkey at Christmas? Where It Came From." September 15, 2023. owtons.com/recipes/why-do-we-eat-turkey-at-christmas/.

Patience Fruit & Co. (website). "9 Things That You May or May Not Know About Cranberries." August 22, 2022. patiencefruitco.com/en/the-patience-club/demystifying-the-cranberry/.

Purdue University College of Agriculture. "Why Ginger Is at the Root of Holiday Traditions." September 18, 2024. ag.purdue.edu/news/2020/12/why-ginger-is-at-the-root-of-holiday-traditions.html.

Raedisch, Linda. *The Old Magic of Christmas: Yuletide Traditions for the Darkest Days of the Year*. Minnesota: Llewellyn Publications, 2013.

Rankel, Kiersten. "What Do Christmas Cactus Flowers Mean?" Greg App (website). June 18, 2024. greg.app/christmas-cactus-flowers/.

Ratsch, Christian, and Claudia Miller-Ebeling. *Pagan Christmas: The Plants, Spirits and Rituals at the Origins of Yuletide*. Vermont: Inner Traditions International, 2006.

Rent-a-Christmas (website). "Garland Galore: A History of Festive Foliage and Christmas." September 18, 2024. rent-a-christmas.com/blog/article/garland-galore-a-history-of-festive-foliage-christmas.

Ricardo Cuisine (website). "Rosemary: Christmas Herb." September 18, 2024. ricardocuisine.com/en/articles/the-ingredient/194-rosemary-christmas-herb.

Rickman, Catherine. "12 Grapes at Midnight: Spain's Unique New Year's Eve Tradition." Food Republic (website). June 12, 2023. foodrepublic.com/1296466/12-grapes-at-midnight/.

Rousseau, Dérick, and Veronica Ann Hislop. "The History of Candy Canes and Why They Taste so Cool." The Conversation (website). September 18, 2024. theconversation.com/the-history-of-candy-canes-and-why-they-taste-so-cool-128036.

Seed World Group (website). "Paperwhites Are a Christmas and Chinese New Year Staple." January 2, 2024. seedworld.com/us/2022/12/23/paperwhites-are-a-christmas-and-chinese-new-year-staple-2/.

Stovell, Fernando. "The Nutty Tradition: Chestnuts: A Global Christmas Delicacy." Fernando Stovell (website). September 18, 2024. cheffernandostovell.com/the-nutty-tradition-chestnuts-a-global-christmas-delicacy/.

Stritch, Larry. "Plants of the Winter Solstice." USDA Forest Service Department of Agriculture (website). fs.usda.gov/managing-land/wildflowers/plant-of-the-week/winter-solstice.

Sweeton, Deborah and Michael Sweeton. *Christmas Trees & Holiday Greens*. Connecticut: The Lyons Press, 2003.

Thursd (website). "The Uniqueness of Amaryllis for the Christmas Season." December 6, 2023. thursd.com/articles/amaryllis-for-christmas.

Toast (website). "A Brief History of Clementines at Christmas." December 9, 2019. tinyurl.com/bdd7582t.

Tomczak, Sylvia. "The Ancient Roman Origins of Stuffing." Tasting Table (website). November 11, 2022. tastingtable.com/1097922/the-ancient-roman-origins-of-stuffing/.

Trees for Life (website). "Oak Mythology and Folklore." March 5, 2021. treesforlife.org.uk/into-the-forest/trees-plants-animals/trees/oak/oak-mythology-and-folklore/.

Tree2mydoor (website). "Celtic Tree Calendar." September 18, 2024. tree2mydoor.com/pages/information-trees-celtic-tree-calendar.

U'mista Cultural Society Synthescape Art Imaging. "The Tree of Life: Cedar—Education—Living Tradition, the Kwakwaka'wakw Potlatch on the Northwest Coast." September 18, 2024. umistapotlatch.ca/enseignants-education/cours_4_partie_2-lesson_4_part_2-eng.php.

University of Minnesota Extension (website). "Growing and Caring for Amaryllis." September 18, 2024. extension.umn.edu/houseplants/amaryllis#selecting-bulbs-858660.

USDA Forest Service. "New Research Reveals Major Difference in Genomes of American and Chinese Chestnuts." Phys.org (website). January 15, 2024. phys.org/news/2024-01-reveals-major-difference-genomes-american.html.

VanZile, Jon, and Peg Aloi. "How to Grow and Care for Kalanchoe." The Spruce (website). September 17, 2024. thespruce.com/growing-kalanchoe-plants-1902982.

Wasserman, Pam. "World Population by Religion: A Global Tapestry of Faith." Population Education (website). January 12, 2024. populationeducation.org/world-population-by-religion-a-global-tapestry-of-faith/.

Wisconsin Horticulture (website). "Ginger, Zingiber Officinale." September 18, 2024. hort.extension.wisc.edu/articles/ginger-zingiber-officinale/.

———. "Mistletoe." September 18, 2024. hort.extension.wisc.edu/articles/mistletoe/.

Wright, Andy. "Mistletoe Is a Parasitic, Explosive Plant That Maybe You Shouldn't Stand Underneath." Atlas Obscura (website). October 16, 2019. atlasobscura.com/articles//mistletoe-is-a-parasitic-explosive-plant-that-maybe-you-shouldnt-stand-underneath.

XpatAthens (website). "Why Greeks Break a Pomegranate on New Year's Day." December 20, 2023. xpatathens.com/living-in-athens/taste-experience/greek-traditions/item/6320-why-greeks-break-a-pomegranate-on-new-year-s-day.

INDEX